Readers' praise for Melanie Chitwood's previous book,
What a Husband Needs from His Wife

"God has used your book to transform my mind, my thinking, and my heart. It is nothing short of a miracle that God has made such major changes so quickly. My husband and I are reaping so many benefits. We are experiencing each other anew and enjoying just being together."

"Your book has changed my life. We were very close to divorce, but I credit your book with changing my whole perspective enough to save our marriage."

"Regardless of how long a couple has been married, newlyweds or married 52 years like us, they can benefit from the biblical and practical ideas in *What a Husband Needs from His Wife*."

"The very situations I have struggled with for years were addressed in *What a Husband Needs from His Wife*. As I have prayed and applied the principles in your book, I am seeing my marriage transformed right before my very eyes."

"Your book came into my life in God's perfect timing. I have highlighted, underlined, and circled so many words throughout the book. It has been like you wrote the book for me."

"After reading *What a Husband Needs from His Wife*, a deep, unconditional love for my husband has overtaken me. For the first time during our marriage, instead of telling God about all my husband's faults, I have begun to thank the Lord for him, and I have asked God to change my faults. Miraculously, we now have the same love and affection that we had when we were dating."

What a Wife Needs from Her Husband

Melanie Chitwood

HARVEST HOUSE PUBLISHERS

EUGENE, OREGON

Unless otherwise indicated, all Scripture quotations are taken from the New American Standard Bible®, © 1960, 1962, 1963, 1968, 1971, 1972, 1973, 1975, 1977, 1995 by The Lockman Foundation. Used by permission. (www .Lockman.org)

Verses marked NLT are taken from the *Holy Bible,* New Living Translation, copyright © 1996, 2004. Used by permission of Tyndale House Publishers, Inc., Wheaton, IL 60189 USA. All rights reserved.

Verses marked MSG are taken from The Message. Copyright © by Eugene H. Peterson 1993, 1994, 1995, 1996, 2000, 2001, 2002. Used by permission of NavPress Publishing Group.

Verses marked NIV are taken from the Holy Bible, New International Version®. NIV®. Copyright © 1973, 1978, 1984 by Biblica, Inc.™ Used by permission of Zondervan. All rights reserved.

Verses marked AMP are taken from The Amplified Bible, Copyright © 1954, 1958, 1962, 1964, 1965, 1987 by The Lockman Foundation. All rights reserved. Used by permission. (www.Lockman.org)

Cover by Left Coast Design, Portland, Oregon

Cover photo © Yuri Arcurs/iStockphoto

WHAT A WIFE NEEDS FROM HER HUSBAND
Copyright © 2010 by Melanie Chitwood
Published by Harvest House Publishers
Eugene, Oregon 97402
www.harvesthousepublishers.com

Library in Congress Cataloging-in-Publication Data

Chitwood, Melanie
What a wife needs from her husband / Melanie Chitwood.
p. cm.
ISBN 978-0-7369-2556-3 (pbk.)
1. Husbands—Religious life.   2. Marriage—Religious aspects—Christianity   I. Title
BV4528.3C45 2010
248.8'—dc22
                                                    2009017191

All rights reserved. No part of this publication may be reproduced, stored in a retrieval system, or transmitted in any form or by any means—electronic, mechanical, digital, photocopy, recording, or any other—except for brief quotations in printed reviews, without the prior permission of the publisher.

Printed in the United States of America

10 11 12 13 14 15 16 17 18 / VP-NI / 10 9 8 7 6 5 4 3 2 1

Acknowledgments

In Him all things hold together.
COLOSSIANS 1:17

To Scott, Zachary, and Tyler, my favorite three people in the world, I am blessed beyond measure to be your wife and mother.

To Amy, Holly, Kelly, and Mandy, thank you for holding me up. I couldn't do life without you.

To Ron and Catherine, so many of the ideas in this book reflect the blessing of your influence in my life.

To the Vaughans, thank you for the open invitation to the lake house and for being my biggest fans.

To the Chitwood and Stubbs family members, thank you for your amazing support this year.

To my Proverbs 31 sisters in Christ, you inspire me to live boldly for Christ.

To the men and women who shared their stories in this book, may God's richest blessings fall on your marriages.

To Harvest House Publishers, especially to Gene Skinner, it is an honor to partner with you in bringing God's message to marriages.

Contents

1

The Starting Point

When I wrote my first book, *What a Husband Needs from His Wife*, I really wanted to write *What a Wife Needs from Her Husband*. I thought I could have finished that book in a week. Not surprisingly, many other women I talked to readily agreed to give me input for that book. And now, here I am with what I've always wanted—a chance to share with husbands what wives need—but now I feel almost paralyzed by several reservations I have about writing this book. I realize that they may be the same reservations you have about reading it, so let's take a moment to clear the air.

First, I'm married to a man who does not like to be told what to do. You probably don't either. Truth be told, no one likes to be told what to do. So as you read this book, please don't think of it as a woman telling you what to do, because that's not what this is about. I want to focus on what God says about marriage, not what I say or any other woman says. I will, however, share some stories from my own marriage and from other couples' relationships to give you ideas about living out God's principles.

Second, perhaps you've read other marriage books but felt that they really didn't help that much. Maybe that's true, but then again, maybe you read the book but didn't really apply the principles. Will you try again? An investment in your marriage is never wasted.

Third, I'm hesitant to write because I'm not sure how this book got into your hands. Maybe you saw it on the bookshelf, and in a real desire to improve your marriage, you picked it up. Thank you. My prayer is that this book will open your heart to God and to your wife. Maybe someone shared this book with you because it really helped his marriage. I hope that's the case. I hope you will find practical applications that will help you have the kind of marriage you really desire. And I hope you can encourage other married couples too.

And I imagine you might be reading this book because your wife asked you to. Now, if that's the case, how did she go about asking you to read it? Did she set it beside your nightstand and not say a word? Did she suggest gently that this book might be good for your marriage? Or did she present the book to you with the implication that you have no idea what she needs, so read the book, for Pete's sake! Or worse, maybe your wife suggested with anger and resentment that since you have been clueless for so long, she would do just about anything to make you understand what she needs.

Even if your wife presented this book to you in a less than tender fashion, will you read it anyway? Will you consider the possibility that you and your wife have spent years together with unspoken and unmet needs? Will you entertain the idea that her anger might mask a broken heart? Will you consider that your wife may be desperate for you to understand a little more of what she needs?

One more thing. As you read this book, you may occasionally think, *What about my wife? She's not necessarily doing everything she should be doing.* I'm sure that's true, but I'm asking you to focus on yourself for now. If your wife is open to the idea, consider inviting her to read *What a Husband Needs from His Wife* while you read this book. Both have study guides at the end that can help you have some great talks with your wife.

Now that I've cleared the air a bit, I hope you'll read this book with an open mind and open heart. God called you to be your wife's husband because He knew you would love her best.

Getting Started

Our family recently took a trip to Atlanta, Georgia, where Scott and I met, fell in love, became engaged, and began our marriage. We enjoyed telling our two sons stories about our early days of dating and marriage. We showed them Open Campus High School (where we both taught), the path where we took our first walk, Buck's restaurant (where we ate out almost weekly), and the house in nearby Decatur, where we lived when first married. I'm sure we enjoyed reliving our memories more than our sons enjoyed hearing about them.

Teaching at the same school, Scott and I saw each other daily. We tried to keep our relationship low-key and under wraps, but the anticipation of seeing him at school each day made me hurry to get up and get to work! I constantly thought of errands to run that required me to walk past his classroom so I could get at least a glimpse of him.

We were married about a year after meeting, and like most newlyweds, we were crazy in love. We were really not thinking too much about what marriage would entail other than happiness, companionship, and lots of sex. To be more accurate, we agreed that the destination in our marriage journey was happiness. We were on different paths, however, leading to that destination. Not surprisingly, my path included many rest stops of tender moments, talking, and togetherness. Meanwhile, Scott's path to marital happiness included a sexual interlude about every ten feet.

We would not have been able to articulate this at the time, but it soon became apparent that we had different ideas about marriage. The first few years of our marriage were filled with a lot more fighting than happiness. We loved each other, and we both loved God, but we just could not figure out how to be married. We kept doing what we were doing, taking occasional stabs at meeting each other's needs and making one another happy, but we usually missed the mark.

Before getting married, my life was rich and full with my teaching job, church involvement, and many close friendships. Once I was married, I kept up with all these activities and friendships. My lifestyle didn't change drastically except that I was living with this man who frustrated me way too much.

Though I had plenty going on in my life apart from Scott, his schedule was even busier. Along with working as a high school math teacher, Scott coached three sports and was also going to flight school part-time. These separate activities left little time for us to spend together.

One Friday night in our first year of marriage, we had planned to go to dinner and a movie—our favorite once-a-week date before marriage. Our plan was that Scott would pick me up and then we'd go out. Because we both had busy schedules and spent a lot of time apart, I was really looking forward to some couple time.

As I was getting ready, Scott called to tell me that he was running late and I would have to meet him at the restaurant. I went ballistic! I didn't want to meet him; I wanted to be picked up, just as if we had been dating rather than married. I angrily told him, "Just forget it. If it's too much trouble for you to take me out, don't bother." He was shocked at my response, which to him seemed extreme and irrational. We argued some more as he tried to convince me to meet him. I stuck to my stubborn ways and refused. By the end of the conversation, we were definitely not going out on a date, and we were also spitting mad at one another.

Unfortunately, our marriage ebbed and flowed like this for many years. We thought if we could just make a few tweaks, our marriage would surely become more satisfying. Throw in some dates here, some sex there, and we'd have a great marriage. Obviously we were wrong because we continued to have a strife-filled marriage. We always made up because we were sorry, we both loved each other, and we longed for peace. Nevertheless, we continued to be constantly frustrated with one another. We were each thinking the same thing about the other person: *You just don't get it!*

Trusting God

Actually, we were right about that. Both of us didn't get it. Several years into our marriage, Scott and I knew we needed a new marriage playbook. The one we were following was not working, and we experienced one losing season after another. Why did we keep repeating the same mistakes over and over? What we did in our marriage wasn't having the results we wanted, so one would think we wouldn't keep using the same ineffective plays. Our pattern wasn't logical, but we didn't seem to notice. We were caught up in emotions, both of us working hard each day at our jobs but not taking much time to evaluate our marriage and what it needed.

Several years into our marriage, we were finally worn-out from the constant strife. I had become a volcano of anger, spewing frustration and disappointment onto Scott. In return, he felt hopeless, so he either attacked me in return or withdrew to defend himself from my constant anger. I was completely focused on Scott's shortcomings but blind to my own. By this time, however, we had two young sons, and we really didn't want them to grow up in an environment of constant conflict.

Crying one night after another fight, I finally realized that I was the one who needed to change. As long as I stayed mad at Scott for not changing, we would get nowhere. We'd keep doing the same things with the same unsatisfying results.

As I sat in the recliner and told God about my misery, He led me to several verses that turned on a lightbulb in my mind. I saw that my choices could make a huge impact in our marriage. One of the passages was Proverbs 3:5-6: "Trust in the LORD with all your heart and do not lean on your own understanding. In all your ways acknowledge Him, and He will make your paths straight." These were some of the first verses I had memorized many years earlier as a young Christian, but applying these to my marriage brought new depths of meaning. That day was a turning point for me and for our marriage. No longer was I going to focus on the changes I thought Scott should make to improve our marriage. Instead, I knew I had to focus on my own choices and trust God with my marriage.

Trusting God with my marriage included surrendering to God's principles instead of relying on my own ideas. It included confessing my pride and defensiveness to God and to Scott. No longer would I try to change Scott; instead, I prayed for both of us to be the kind of people God wanted us to be. As I trusted my marriage to God and began to apply godly principles to our marriage, our relationship started to change, and we began to have the kind of marriage we both longed for, one of peace, unity, and laughter.

Trusting God is the starting point for building the kind of marriage God has planned for you. Trusting means surrendering, yielding, and changing. Surrendering may sound more like defeat, weakness, and failure, situations the world would tell a man to avoid at all costs. However, your standards for being the kind of husband God wants you to be must always come from God's Word, not the world's example and pressures.

From the Inside Out

The marriage God wants for you will develop only as your heart is transformed. I found this verse when writing my first book about a husband's needs. I want to include it in this book as well because it captures perfectly what God is looking for in spouses: "The king's heart is like channels of water in the hand of the LORD; He turns it wherever He wishes" (Proverbs 21:1).

God wants a husband to be yielded to Him so He can transform that man from the inside out. Unless you are willing to let God change your heart, reading this book will be no different from reading a secular self-help book. Self-help focuses on the obvious: self. Depending on yourself rather than God's power working through you to be the kind of husband God wants you to be just won't work. You'll get worn out and frustrated as you rely on your own efforts. God wants you to seek Him, and He'll work through you with His power, love, and grace to love your wife for Him.

Butch and Mandy Ferguson have been married 22 years. Butch describes how he came to the point of surrendering his marriage to God.

> One day, I looked at a huge oak tree that had broken in half during a windstorm the night before. The tree had looked healthy on the outside, but it was actually rotting on the inside. Sounds like the way my marriage used to be. It appeared healthy to others, but it was decaying, just like that old oak tree. Deep down, I loved Mandy and didn't want to lose her, but I didn't know how to love her. She wanted to go to counseling, so I finally worked up the nerve to contact our church and make an appointment.
>
> Mandy stated that she had simply fallen out of love with me over the years because of our lack of communication on key issues. I wondered how we could have let our marriage get to this point. With this in mind, I embraced our counseling program. Our marriage began improving, but we continued to have ups and downs.
>
> I was about to leave on a business trip one day when Mandy and I had a serious blowout. I left town with a heavy heart, and Satan was filling me with lies that things would never change between us and that I should just live with or without it. I was in my hotel room by ten p.m., and I called home. Mandy was quiet and to the point, and she

wasted no words answering my questions about the kids, their day, and the like. She added nothing else and eventually hung up on me because she was just fed up with the conversation, with me, and with life.

At that moment, I realized I couldn't fix my marriage. I had tried, but it just wasn't working. I stood in my room and cried out to God, *Why can't we just love each other and get along?* Instantly, I knew the answer. All this time, I was the one who was trying to fix things, and I knew deep inside that it was really up to God to repair our marriage, so I put it in His hands through prayer. *God, I can't fix our marriage. I've been trying for 16 years, but it's still broken.* It was up to God as I surrendered my life and my marriage.

To me, surrendering is like admitting defeat, and as a guy, I hate to get beat. But that night, *surrender* became part of my vocabulary. I surrendered our marriage to God and asked that He give me direction in my life, especially in my marriage. I prayed that Mandy would allow Christ to live through her and begin to heal the hurts that I had caused over the years. I trusted God to change us in His perfect timing. I was filled with hope—I couldn't wait to get home.

We Go Together

To be the kind of husband God wants you to be, you must turn to His Word to learn principles of being a godly husband. Let's look in Genesis to learn from the first marriage God created. As we read the creation story in Genesis 1–2, we see that after six days of creating all sorts of marvels, land and light and creatures, God "saw all that He had made, and behold, it was very good" (Genesis 1:31). There is one time, however, in this creation process that God chooses to say something is "not good." After making Adam, God states, "It is not good for the man to be alone" (Genesis 2:18). In all the millions of things God created, He said only one item needed some more work!

God knew that Adam's life would be better with a companion. God planned that this person would make Adam no longer alone. Dear husband, God knows you too need a companion. God's plan is for a husband and wife to need one another and to complement one another.

My husband has many wonderful qualities: a strong work ethic, muscular shoulders from years of playing basketball, and the ability to repair any household item. Of course, my list of his wonderful traits could continue. I'm sure your wife could also make a list of your admirable qualities. Nevertheless, God says that husbands need a companion. In Genesis 2:18, God calls that companion a helper: "I will make him a helper suitable for him." All the days of marriage allow a husband and wife to embrace each other's strengths and weaknesses and to see how they can complement one another. Recognizing your need of a helper will strengthen your marriage. Resisting your partner's help will tear your marriage apart.

Oneness

Let's continue to look at Genesis to uncover more of God's design for marriage. When Adam finished naming the animals, one thing was abundantly clear:

> For Adam there was not found a helper suitable for him. So the LORD God caused a deep sleep to fall upon the man, and he slept; then He took one of his ribs and closed up the flesh at that place. The LORD God fashioned into a woman the rib which He had taken from the man, and brought her to the man (Genesis 2:20-22).

All the other creatures were made from the ground, but Adam's companion, Eve, came from his very own body. Scripture says in Genesis 2:24, "and they shall become one flesh." Oneness is vital to a marriage. Oneness, or being "one flesh," includes not only physically becoming one but also much more. Being one flesh includes physical oneness along with emotional, spiritual, and mental oneness. God intends husbands and wives to know each other and be known in the most intimate of ways.

Oneness is one of the treasures of marriage but also one of its challenges. We long for intimacy, but it doesn't necessarily come easily. Oneness requires husbands and wives to lay down their rights, entitlement, freedom, independence, and expectations. Let's look at some real-life examples of how we create oneness.

- When you were single, you may have spent almost every fall weekend in the woods hunting. In addition, perhaps your job required you to work out of town a few nights a week. But now you are married, so you choose not to go hunting every weekend because you don't want to be away from your wife so frequently. You prioritize spending time with your wife.

- You're sitting on the couch watching TV when your five-year-old comes into the room to kiss you goodnight. Instead of sitting there on the couch, waiting for your wife to tuck your little one in, you get up and do the bedtime routine.

- You're having dinner with your wife when a really attractive waitress comes to take your order. You make sure your eyes don't linger on the waitress as she walks away.

These are just a few examples of everyday choices that can help stitch together the fabric of oneness in your marriage. Just as easily, your choices can tear apart oneness. For example, you go out with the guys instead of going to that chick flick your wife's been wanting you to take her to. You don't make a point of saying "I love you" anymore. You forget her birthday or your anniversary. Oneness means that your wife deserves the best of you—your best time, energy, and attention. God chose you to be your wife's husband, and as you love her the way God wants you to, you'll be the husband she needs.

The moment we are married, we become one flesh, and then we

work out our oneness all the days of our marriage. Husbands and wives must constantly guard, protect, and nurture their oneness because marriages face countless attacks each day. The values of our world are completely contrary to God's ideas of marriage. The home you grew up in and your friendships might not have provided you with examples of how to be a godly husband. When you don't have good examples, knowing how to act can be difficult. In the pages of this book you will find many stories of husbands just like you who are learning to live out God's principles of trusting Him, surrendering to Him, and honoring oneness in marriage.

Willing to Change

As I look back at the first years of my marriage, I see that Scott and I were not embracing our new oneness at all. We were simply living by the old rules of our single days. For example, the time we spent involved with friends, hobbies, or professional advancement often showed that those things remained higher priorities than being together. As we eventually began to trust God with our marriage, we started making different choices that strengthened the oneness in our marriage.

Living out God's principles for marriage requires a lot of a husband and wife. You can't just keep on doing what you've been doing. Marriage requires you to change, to lay down your wishes and yield to your wife's, to sacrifice some of your own dreams and help her fulfill hers, and to come alongside her in the daily ins and outs of life. Husbands and wives must learn to focus on *we* rather than *me*.

So marriage will require you to change. Will these changes be easy? Some changes will, but many will not. Think of it this way. Remember the days of jeans that were not prewashed? (If you're too young to remember, surely you've heard about those days!) I remember wearing the stiffest, most unyielding Wrangler jeans. Whether you were a girl or boy, these were the cool jeans to have, but they were far from comfortable. These new jeans were so stiff they could almost stand by themselves. Gradually, however, with days of playing and running, those jeans began to fit just right. Soon those Wrangler jeans became my favorites, the ones I always wanted to wear.

The changes you make in your marriage may feel like those brand-new Wrangler jeans—stiff, uncomfortable, and hard to wear at first. Eventually, however, the habits you practice in your marriage will become a part of your character. Your new habits will become your first reactions, just as those new jeans one day became perfectly worn-in and the first ones I reached for.

Gary Smalley, a Christian counselor, writer, and speaker who has become renowned for his wisdom on marriage and family, describes some of his early steps toward oneness in his marriage. He explains what happened with his wife, Norma, as he humbled himself before her and before God.

> "Could you forgive me for the way I've treated you?" I asked. "I'm willing to change. I'll really plan on changing."
>
> "Sure, I've heard that song before," she said skeptically.
>
> I didn't know how long it would take for me to reform. But I knew the next time someone called right before dinner, I would have to ask, "Is this an emergency, or can we work it out tomorrow?" I had to show her I really meant business about valuing her and meeting her needs *first*.
>
> I *wanted* to tell her she was the most important person in my life. I really *wanted* to feel that way. At first I didn't have those feelings, but I *wanted* to have them. As I tried to make her more important to me than anyone else, I soon began to *feel* she was top priority...
>
> My pride was broken, my ego bruised, and my feelings wounded in numerous falls from marital harmony during the first two years of living these principles. Because I tried so hard to make it work, Norma finally believed I was earnest in my endeavor to change. But it took two years to

convince her—and it may take you that long to convince
your wife.[1]

I appreciate Smalley's honesty in admitting that his marriage took
two years to begin to change directions. To make the necessary changes
in our marriages, we need to commit to a new way of life and not
look for a quick fix. I have no doubt that you will see some immediate positive results, but if you've had years of a troubled marriage, be
prepared to reap the harvest over time.

Assess Your Own Marriage

Let's pause for a minute. I've told you some of my marriage story
and stories from a few other couples. Now I want you to stop and consider your own marriage story. Maybe you can relate to the conflicts
in my marriage because your marriage is characterized by more strife
than peace. Maybe you're thinking, *I don't get it. I don't get my wife,
and I don't know if I ever will.*

Or maybe you're thinking, *Wait a minute. I'm not sure I even need
to read this book. I already have a pretty good marriage.*

Perhaps you started off strong in your marriage, but over the years,
the daily stresses of jobs, bills, and children have accumulated, and
you really don't like the path your marriage is on.

Maybe your marriage is pretty good, but deep down inside you
think God has something more in mind for you than a marriage that
is just "fine."

Or perhaps your marriage has reached such a state of hopelessness and bitterness that you're not really sure you even want to stay
married.

I am not a marriage expert, but I know the One who is: our heavenly
Father, the One who created marriage. Whatever positive or negative
thoughts you have about your marriage, God knows exactly where you
are; He knows all about your thoughts and feelings in your marriage.

The good news is that God has good plans for you, and they include good plans for your marriage.

As you apply God's principles to your marriage and follow the ideas in this book, you'll discover how to trust God with your marriage. And as you become the man God wants you to be, you'll also become the husband your wife needs.

I believe men want to love their wives the way God wants them to, but often they're not sure what that means. Consider this book as a window into your wife's heart. As you read about God's principles and as other couples share their stories of successes and failures, let them point you to God, to His principles of marriage, and to your wife.

Holy Ground

In this book I'm going to suggest some changes you can make in your marriage. I've already mentioned some in this chapter, and before we go any further I want to give you a fresh perspective from which to view this transformation. It's a perspective I learned when I read about Moses, one of my favorite people in Scripture.

Honestly, I used to think of Moses as one of the most unlikely people for a contemporary woman to relate to. Several years ago, however, while reading through the Bible chronologically, I ended up spending a whole lot of time reading Exodus and Deuteronomy. I began to ask God to reveal Himself to me in the pages of these books and the heart of this man Moses. When I did, Moses became real to me—and not just as an old man with a beard making loud and scary proclamations.

In Exodus 3, Moses is an ordinary shepherd, doing his everyday job of tending sheep, when he encounters our extraordinary God. Moses sees that a "bush was burning with fire, yet the bush was not consumed" (Exodus 3:2), so he goes to investigate this unusual phenomenon. Unexpectedly, God speaks to Moses, saying, "Do not come near here; remove your sandals from your feet, for the place on which you are standing is holy ground" (verse 5).

We can imagine God saying the same thing to us about our marriages: *Take off your shoes; you are on holy ground.* We may see the ground of our marriages as joyful, ho-hum, or quite challenging, but God sees it as it really is: holy.

When we understand that marriage is sacred, we see that who pays the bills, how often we have sex, and how we raise the kids are not simply matters of convenience. The daily activities in a marriage provide opportunities for us to encounter God. We are on holy ground. We'll talk in this book about how to live out the daily ins and outs of marriage, but at the same time I want to ask you to view all of marriage as a place where we meet God, let Him take hold of our hearts, and allow Him to transform us so we look more like Him.

PRAYER GUIDE

Dear Lord,

Thank you for my wife and my marriage. I want the marriage You want me to have, and I am willing to do whatever You want me to do. I surrender my heart to You and ask that You turn it in the right direction. I confess that at times I have been willful, prideful, and stubborn. I've too quickly pointed out my wife's faults while ignoring my own shortcomings. Lord, work through me to love and treasure my wife for You. Give me the desire to change and the strength to be the kind of husband You want me to be. Then I know I'll be the husband my wife needs. Lord, give me Your perspective of marriage, a perspective that sees my marriage as holy ground, a place where You can change my character to be more like Yours. Amen.

2

Be the Man

Two years ago Scott told me he wanted to pursue his passion of youth sports. He was already coaching community teams, so I imagined this might involve more coaching on the weekends. But I thought, *If that's where Scott feels God leading him, I'll support him.*

I pictured Scott coaching during his free time, but Scott's dreams surpassed anything I could imagine. He told me his friend Ron Esser called him to share his idea of building a gym. Scott told Ron, "Let's do it."

All I could think of was a slight variation of the line from the movie *Field of Dreams:* "If you build it, they will come." I jokingly shared this thought with Scott, laughing at my cleverness and his crazy idea. When he didn't laugh along with me, I soon realized he was completely serious.

We began months of praying, seeking God's will, discussing the idea with each other, and dreaming with our partners, the Essers.

We took a giant leap of faith, and both couples decided, "We're in." Carolina Courts, an indoor gym with five basketball and volleyball courts, recently opened for business.

Even now as I'm standing in our new facility, sometimes I think, *How did I ever get here?* I know a whole lot about Barbie dolls, shopping, and books, but the world of sports was pretty foreign to me—until I met Scott. Because I love Scott, I've entered into his world of sports. I just never imagined such a big leap!

When Scott first shared the dream God was planting in his heart, I should have known immediately that it would be a big dream, for that's how God has wired him. His adventuresome spirit is attractive to, but it also is very different from me. I am not adventuresome. I don't really like to be stretched or to step out of my comfort zone. Truthfully, I like to get life all figured out and settle in for some predictability. That's why even now, as I stand in our facility, it feels surreal. I have to remind myself, *This is our gym.*

How did God get me to a place where I was willing to jump off the cliff with Scott, not knowing where we would land? The answer is simple: I trust Scott. I trust him because he's been faithful and loving for 18 years. More importantly, I trust him because I know he has a solid relationship with the Lord. Women thrive on security, and one of the most secure feelings we women can have comes from knowing our husbands have solid relationships with the Lord. As we continue in this chapter, we'll look at some practical ways to seek the Lord. We'll also look at why this is important to wives.

First Things First

Trusting God with our marriages means seeking Him first. God clearly tells us how to order and prioritize our lives: "Seek first His kingdom and His righteousness, and all these things will be added to you" (Matthew 6:33). This instruction provides the foundation for a marriage built on God's principles.

God also tells us to seek Him wholeheartedly: "You will seek Me and find Me when you search for Me with all your heart" (Jeremiah 29:13). What are you wholeheartedly devoted to? One way to truthfully answer this question is to consider who or what gets your time, energy, and finances. Is it your job, hobby, recreation, friends, extended family, wife, kids, home, yard...?

No doubt you often feel the pull and pressure of many responsibilities. How can you fulfill all these responsibilities and be the husband your wife needs? It seems like a tall order, doesn't it?

Imagine you have a home with several acres of land. You've been working outside for about an hour, and you stop for a few minutes to get a drink of water. As you stand surveying your property, you see many reminders of the various responsibilities in your life. The flower beds out front, which you planted for your wife, need weeding and mulching. The yard hasn't been mowed or edged in two weeks. The swing set for your kids is showing wear and tear and will require paint soon. Your shed is a mess inside, and you wish you had time to organize it. As much as you love working outside, assessing what needs to be done—by you and you alone—suddenly makes you feel weary. How are you possibly going to have time to do all of this?

Then you notice a man sitting on a bench in the back area of your property. You head his way to say hello, thinking he must be your neighbor, who has an open invitation to enjoy your yard. But as you approach, you see he's someone you don't know. He waves to you to beckon you over to him. When you near him, you see that he is dressed as if he too has been working in the yard. He's wearing a hat with a wide brim to protect him from the sun. The knees of his overalls are covered with dirt. His gardening gloves rest beside him on the bench.

The gardener doesn't say a word, but smiles warmly as he offers you a tall glass of ice water. You reach for it, thank him, and then lift it to drink. As you taste the water, you find it's the most amazing water you've ever had. How could simple water be so good? Even though you gulp and gulp, the drink doesn't end. Finally, you finish drinking, and you have never felt so satisfied. Your thirst is completely quenched. You feel an amazing sense of peace. The weariness you felt earlier is gone.

God alone satisfies us this way. Jesus is the living water (John 4:10). He invites you to drink deeply. When you do, you will no longer thirst. As you choose to be the husband your wife needs, you will sometimes feel overwhelmed. You will realize that other people's needs are more than you can handle. Let God fill you with His living water as you seek Him with all your heart. Then, as you love your wife, you'll be giving what the Lord has already filled you with—Himself.

Seeking God

As you read this book, remember not to approach it as a giant to-do list. It includes many practical applications, but your marriage will change because of your relationship with the Lord and from the inside out.

As you seek God, you will sense more and more that God loves you—completely, unconditionally, and without reservation or hesitation. His love is lavish, as He sacrificially expressed by His death on a cross.

God wants you to know His love and to be sure of it once and for all. That was the apostle Paul's desire for his readers as well:

> I pray that from his glorious, unlimited resources he will empower you with inner strength through his Spirit. Then Christ will make his home in your hearts as you trust in him. Your roots will grow down into God's love and keep you strong. And may you have the power to understand, as all God's people should, how wide, how long, how high, and how deep his love is. May you experience the love of Christ, though it is too great to understand fully. Then you will be made complete with all the fullness of life and power that comes from God (Ephesians 3:16-19 NLT).

Make this prayer yours by personalizing it: *I pray that from Your glorious, unlimited resources, You will empower me with inner strength through Your Spirit...*

Is Christ at home in your heart? Maybe at one time you committed your life to Christ, and you have continued to walk hand in hand with the Lord. May the words of this book encourage you to continue your journey. Or maybe you've wandered, and you know that you've gotten far away from God's path. You can be sure that God can *always* find you and rescue you with His love. His plan always has been and always will be to love you and rescue you regardless of your circumstances.

If you've never asked God into your heart, let today be the day when you pray for Christ to fill your life. You can pray a prayer like the one that follows, or you can form your own prayer by simply expressing your desire to know Jesus as your Lord, Savior, and Friend.

> Jesus, I don't know everything about You or about being Your child, but I know enough to know that I want to be in a relationship with You. I know that I'm a sinner and that I need Your forgiveness. Thank You for Your death on a cross, which paid the price for my sins. Thank You for Your resurrection, which empowers me to live a new life. I want my life to be about following You. Amen.

Now you can be assured that from this moment forward you are God's child and nothing will ever change that. All of heaven rejoices with you. Tell some people—especially your wife and closest friends—that you've become a child of God.

Seeking God with all your heart is similar to any other relationship or commitment—it will require you to invest your time. One way to do that is to have a quiet time each day, a time that you dedicate to being with God. In these moments, you get to know God as your Friend, Master, and Savior. God tells us, "Cease striving and know that I am God" (Psalm 46:10). Another translation states, "Be still, and know that I am God" (NIV). When a body is physically still, the mind is more likely to be still and to focus on Him.

A quiet time can include a time of talking to God in prayer. Your prayers don't have to be formal or carefully worded. Just speak to God from your heart—that's what He wants to hear. Your honest and complete vulnerability is what God calls humility, the opposite of pride. When you're overwhelmed with your job, tell God. When you're having a hard time responding to your wife's needs, tell God. When you have a great day with your kids playing softball, tell God. When you're struck with the beauty of a cold fall night, tell God. When you're sorry for your hurtful words, tell God. Sometimes I like to think of prayer as praising God, thanking God, confessing my sins, and praying for others. The important thing is to turn to Him with honesty and sincerity.

Continue to talk to God throughout the day—as you work, as you drive your car, when you don't know what to do, when you do know what to do, and as you approach home and prepare to interact with your family. Maintain an ongoing conversation with God. "Rejoice always; pray without ceasing; in everything give thanks; for this is God's will for you in Christ Jesus" (1 Thessalonians 5:16-18). This is what Jesus means when He tells us to abide in Him (John 15:4). God's desire is to be constantly in relationship with us, to love us, and to work through us.

Don't forget to listen for God's answers. At first, listening to God can be one of the hardest things you ever do. Keep on keeping on. In time you'll begin to recognize His voice—not audibly, but as an impression in your heart. You'll begin to have a sense of "I know that I know." And it will not be a sense of determination to be right or to have things work out the way you want them. It will be the sense of knowing this is what God wants. Eventually you'll be sure because you know that your heart is surrendered to Him. You don't have to be stressed-out about hearing God's voice. He wants you to hear Him and promises that you will: "My sheep hear my voice, and I know them, and they follow Me" (John 10:27).

God's Word

So much of what God wants to say to us He's already written to us in the Bible, His Word. God's Word will speak to your life now, for it is living and active. Do you read your Bible? If you don't have a Bible translation you can understand, go to a Christian bookstore or online to find one. The *Life Application Study Bible* is filled with practical notes in translations you can easily understand.

The timeless truth of God's Word will be your best map as you journey in marriage. Think about going on a road trip. If you're going somewhere new, you consult a map first so you'll be sure to get there. Then along the way you consult it to affirm your route. If you get lost, you consult the map again. Let God's Word be the map you consult over and over again for directions in your marriage.

If you haven't had much practice reading Scripture, it can seem somewhat overwhelming. Let's look at some ideas to get started.

Two books of the Bible I return to over and over are Psalms and Proverbs, both in the Old Testament. Psalms is a book of honesty, praise, and devotion. Every emotion you can think of is found in the book of Psalms. This shows us God wants us to pour out our hearts to Him. Proverbs is a practical book, filled with wisdom and practical instructions for applying our faith to everyday life. Try reading a chapter of Psalms and a chapter of Proverbs each day.

Another idea is to choose a chapter of the New Testament. Read several verses each day and then ask these questions about the passage. You might want to record your answers in a notebook just to help you keep focused.

- What is the main point of this passage? Summarize it using your own words.

- What do you learn about God, Jesus, and the Holy Spirit?

- What lesson can you apply to your everyday life? How does this passage show you how to live as a man of God?

One other idea is to read through the entire Bible in a year. Many Bibles include a yearly reading plan. You might even want to purchase a chronological Bible, which will facilitate reading through the Bible. Whatever approach you take, the most important thing is simply to read God's Word.

Listening to effective Bible teachers will also help you understand God's Word. Read books about growing as a Christian and talk with other Christian men about what you're learning.

Turning to God's Word demonstrates your reliance on God's wisdom, not your own, as you seek to be the husband your wife needs. "He who gives attention to the word will find good, and blessed is he who trusts in the Lord" (Proverbs 16:20). God's Word will continually explain how He wants you to live as a godly man. As you become the man God wants you to be, you'll become the husband your wife needs.

God's Family, the Church

I've heard so many excuses for not going to church and have thought some myself: *I can worship God and pray anywhere; I don't have to be in a church building. Sunday is the only morning I have to sleep in and do whatever I want. Besides, I'm not really getting that much out of church.*

Church is not a building; it's a family of believers and seekers who gather together in one place to worship God. Relationships are key to God. They are the means He uses to work in this world, and even God Himself exists in relationship. God, the Father, exists in a relationship with His Son, Jesus, and His Spirit, the Holy Spirit. When we're in relationship with other believers, we're loved, supported, challenged, embraced, and encouraged to grow to be more like Christ.

Church is the place God created for us to be in relationship with one another. Your involvement in the church is important for you and for other people, and it's important to God, so make it a priority in your life. Way too many women have to go to church without their husbands. Your job is to lead, so be the man. Lead your family each Sunday to church. No more excuses.

God's Kind of Man Cave

Have you heard of a man cave? If you know what this is and have one, you probably now have a grin on your face just thinking about your man cave. In case you're not sure what a man cave is, let me define it.

> **man cave** (măn cāv) n.: An area, such as a basement, work-shop, garage, or shed, where a man can be alone to pursue guy stuff, such as hobbies, sports, or fixing things.

I'm supportive of the idea of a husband having a man cave, but I also see how it can become a dangerous thing if a man uses it to avoid being engaged and connected with his wife and family. That would be just about the furthest thing from what God's Word encourages. It could become a selfish pursuit rather than an occasional refuge.

My husband has found a man cave beyond our front doors, and it's one I think God really smiles on. The only difference is he goes there not to be alone but to join a group of Christian men from our church. In small groups or Bible studies, men can be honest and vulnerable. They can share the ups and downs of life and go away strengthened and encouraged in their journey with Christ.

Scott's group is led by a godly, humorous, and wise leader in our church, Bob Pace. Bob describes the nature of their man cave:

> So what does a spiritual man cave look like? First of all, we wanted a place to be ourselves and to learn how to apply the teachings of Scripture to our lives in such a way that others could see it, feel it, and want it. It needed to be real and to be relevant.
>
> We found our cave in the upstairs conference room in an athletic field house next to the church. A meeting room that

looks and smells the way an athletic meeting room should became our place to hang out and talk about life, God, ourselves. You come as you are, plop into your chair, spread around the room, and feel like you can be yourself.

As men who enjoy discovery and who value the experiences of others, we recognize and embrace what Scriptures say about the way, the truth, and the life given to us in Christ. We further realize that a clear understanding of God's Word, and of the way that men and women of Scripture lived in relationship to it, are essential in finding our way with God. Our goal is to learn to be like Christ and to live in relationship with Him in every aspect of our lives.

So we get together every Sunday at eight a.m. in our meeting place. We come as we are in heart, in soul, and in the way we dress, and we hang out for an hour with other guys who are at the same place in life. We don't look to spill our guts or dribble out our repressed feelings. But we don't hesitate to ask the hard questions and challenge one another with the hard decisions that push our faith. Sometimes we need to see the nail marks and where the spear pierced, sometimes we need to ask for help in our unbelief, sometimes we need to take our faith into action, and sometimes we just want to be quiet and listen.

I asked Scott to explain the benefits of this men's group. Here's what he said: "It's like going to a different universe for an hour. It relaxes and refreshes me. It allows me to realize I'm not alone, that we're in the same battles. None of us is an island."

We are designed to be in relationship with one another. Too many men engage with each other just on the surface. It's easy to talk about jobs, sports, or house improvements. God wants much more of you. Whom can you talk to about your relationships and your journey as a Christian? Maybe God wants you to initiate this kind of friendship, or maybe He wants you to form some new friendships. Pray about it and be open to His leading. Perhaps you can seek out a group at your church or even be the one to start a spiritual man cave.

Be the Man

Your relationship with the Lord matters to your wife. In fact, two-thirds of the wives I surveyed responded that knowing that their husbands had solid relationships with the Lord is one of their three most important needs. Here are a few examples of the variety of ways wives expressed this need:

> "I need him to be in God's Word and in prayer daily."
>
> "I want him to pray with me and the children."
>
> "I feel secure knowing he loves God."

God's Word confirms that your role in the family is to lead. Ephesians 5:23 tells us, "For the husband is the head of the wife, as Christ also is the head of the church." God provides an order within the family to provide harmony and unity. Leading means you establish the direction and set the tone of your family, and you do this with your words and your actions. It means you are the initiator of these things. You probably occasionally think, *I'll change if my wife changes.* But as the leader, you must go first. You must be the initiator of change.

When you look around for an example of spiritual leadership, you are likely to find more ungodly and ineffective models of leadership than godly and effective examples. God's perspective is very different from the world's, isn't it! If you adopt the world's ideas, you might be led to think that being a strong leader means being authoritarian, domineering, controlling, or even demeaning. Telling your wife what to do, making decisions without consulting her, and implying or directly stating that her place is in the home, raising kids, and cooking your dinner are poor examples of leadership, but I've seen men adopt these practices in the name of spiritual leadership.

Some men might even use the Bible verses about submission in their defense. Ephesians 5:22, "Wives, be subject to your own husbands, as to the Lord," clearly instructs wives to submit, but these verses are best understood in context. If we back up one verse, we see that verse 21 tells us to "be subject to one another." God's Word teaches us that we are to be mutually submissive to one another in marriage. God is looking for us to always respond to one another in love and humility, following Christ's example.

You and your wife are partners who have distinct roles. You are not her master; the Lord is. You cannot make your wife submit to your leadership any more than God makes us submit to His authority. That's up to her and to the Holy Spirit's work in her life. She is free to choose how she will respond to you. Too often husbands and wives try to be one another's Holy Spirit. Instead, focus on what God calls you to do—pray for your wife and your marriage, and let God transform her just as He's transforming you.

Leading Means Serving

So what is spiritual leadership? As an effective spiritual leader, you establish the spiritual climate in your family. To know how to do that, look at Jesus' example. He was a servant leader, and that's the kind of leader God wants you to be. "Do nothing from selfishness or empty conceit, but with humility of mind regard one another as more important than yourselves; do not merely look out for your own personal interests, but also for the interests of others" (Philippians 2:3-4). Jesus shows exactly how He wants a man to lead—by serving. Not by demanding his rights, not by expecting his wife to obey him, not with pride or a sense of entitlement. No, just the opposite. With humility, Jesus reached out to those around Him. He attended to others' needs before His own. Jesus came to serve, and you must do the same.

Author Gary Chapman is a husband who has learned to serve his wife. In fact, he states with confidence, "My goal through all these years has been to serve my wife so well that when I'm gone, she won't find another man who'll treat her the way I've treated her. The woman is going to miss me!"[1]

What might servant leadership look like in marriage? Let's consider some examples.

- When you get home from work, take ten minutes to give your wife your undivided attention, before you open the mail, before you check e-mails, and before you turn on the TV.

- If you see your wife is exhausted, cook dinner. A Chinese proverb says, "Talk doesn't cook rice."

- Go to your in-laws for Thanksgiving because your wife wants to.

- Go with your wife to the fabric store, mall, or coffee shop. Have a cheerful attitude the whole time.

- Change the diapers, take the kids outside to play, bathe the kids. Be hands-on in ways that help your wife and at times she especially needs your support.

- Let your wife pick the TV show and hold the remote.

- Go to a chick flick.

- Complete a home repair or house project she's been asking you to finish.

- Suggest she relax by reading a book or taking a bath while you clean up the kitchen. Do this simply because you love her, not because you hope this will lead to sex.

As a servant leader, you put your wife's needs before your own. Whatever is important to her is now important to you. Sometimes you put your own desires on the back burner. Ask God to show you small and big ways to serve your wife, and be on the lookout for His answers. You will probably feel resistance to serving your wife. It might seem unmanly or even passive. But servant leadership is not passive, and it is not the same thing as abdicating your leadership role. Rather, day in and day out, your servant's heart and hands can demonstrate that a true leader leads with humility, just as Jesus did. Jesus' example set the bar for true strength, leadership, and manliness.

Share Your Spiritual Journey

Many men find the whole idea of spiritual leadership intimidating. After all, you know you're a work in process, far from perfect. You feel like you're spiritually stuck in seventh grade while your wife has a PhD in Christianity. Your insecurity might make you feel like hiding your journey with Christ from your wife. Let me tell you a wonderful secret about women: We don't expect our husbands to be perfect. Wives are attracted to husbands who have sincere hearts, who are honest about their shortcomings but nevertheless are willing to stumble along the path with their wives.

So not having all the answers is okay. Being a little uncomfortable taking the lead praying aloud or discussing Scripture is okay. You are responsible, however, to lead by sharing your spiritual journey with your wife and by being the one who gets the ball rolling. You can start being the spiritual leader by serving her and putting her needs before your own, and gradually you can talk more and more about your journey with the Lord.

Guys hate not knowing how to do something, but God is asking you to move out of your comfort zone. When you're in over your head, don't get embarrassed and don't get angry. Take a deep breath and try depending on God, not on yourself. Pray something like this: *God, I want to be the spiritual leader of our family, but I'm not sure what that means. Show me and give me a willing heart and willing hands.*

As you know because you're married, talking is important to most women. We'll discuss communication later, but for now, just remember that your wife needs you to verbalize some of your spiritual journey. It's one way you can help her feel closer to you.

We discussed earlier the importance of God's Word and prayer to your own journey with the Lord. These are also two tools you can use to build a spiritual relationship with your wife. First she needs to see you seeking God on your own. Then you can share what you discover in your times with God. If you've read something in Scripture that excites you, share that with your wife. Scott receives online devotions, and sometimes he forwards those to me. Whatever he forwards to me reveals his heart and where God is working in his life, and we try to share those lessons with each other. You might want to choose a book of the Bible and both read it. A few times per week, or whatever frequency fits your schedule, discuss what you're learning. Also, excellent couples' devotional books are available, and you could try reading one together.

Prayer is just talking to God, but if you've never prayed out loud with someone, you might feel uncomfortable, even with your wife. Will you sound stupid? Will you be putting on a show? Will you stumble over your words?

When Steve and Annie Chapman wrote *What Husbands and Wives Aren't Telling Each Other,* Steve was up-front about his reluctance to pray aloud.

> I still struggle to this day with being immediately willing to pray with my wife. One very good reason that I sometimes balk is because she knows me so well…and God knows me even better. Though I believe they each deeply love me, to be in the presence of both God and Annie at the same time is, to say the least, rather uncomfortable. She sees me when I get upset, for example, and act foolishly. And for sure, God is always watching. Because of that, I am tempted to shut down and remain silent. Yet, I have seen the power of prayer and have learned that I have to be willing to set aside my feelings of shame and humbly bow on the knees of my heart. When I do make that choice, I am never, ever disappointed.[2]

You don't have to worry about finding the right way to pray, and praying aloud gets easier with practice. Begin by making sure you're praying in your own personal quiet time. Your prayers don't have to be long or eloquent; just pray from your heart. The study guide at the end of this book includes a commitment statement at the end of chapter 1. In it, I challenge you to pray for your wife and your marriage every day. Stormie Omartian's book *The Power of a Praying Husband* is a helpful resource. Each chapter guides you to pray about a certain aspect of your wife's life, such as her relationships or her purpose.

You could practice praying aloud by saying a blessing at dinner or a short prayer with your wife before you both start or end your day. To be honest, this took a long time for Scott and me to do. We both prayed privately, but we didn't make a practice of praying together until several years of our marriage had passed. I wish we had learned to do this sooner because I now believe we left our marriage unguarded and open to spiritual attack. As Stormie Omartian explains, "Whatever you don't pray about in your life, you leave up to chance. And that's not good enough when it comes to your marriage."[3]

When a husband prays aloud with his wife, he invites God's power, protection, and love into her life. She feels as if she's been tenderly placed in the hands of the One who loves her most, her heavenly Father. Her husband's prayers make her feel covered and protected from stress, fear, worry, fatigue, and the strain of daily responsibilities. Some women say they feel most loved when their husbands pray for them.

As you share what you're learning from the Lord, you'll meet one of your wife's primary needs—her desire for you to be the spiritual leader—and your marriage will be strengthened.

Why Your Relationship with God Matters to Your Wife

Sometimes I wonder what Noah's wife thought when he told her he was going to build an ark to save their family and some animals from a flood that would destroy all other living creatures. They'd never seen a drop of rain before. Did she tell him he was crazy? Did she make his life miserable because of this dream, or did she support him? I'm not sure. I hope she supported him, but either way, I imagine one day in heaven, Noah's wife and I will have a good talk.

If Scott's dream of building Carolina Courts had come up earlier in our marriage, I would have slammed the door on that dream, but some significant changes have happened in Scott and in me. God has used the past years to transform our hearts and draw us both closer to Him and to each other.

When Scott began to share his dream of building Carolina Courts, I trusted him. I know Scott's heart belongs to God, so Scott has my heart as well. This is so important for you to understand. Your wife wants to trust you, wants to follow your leadership, and wants to submit to you. You can help her do what God wants her to do by being a man after God's own heart. When she is assured your heart belongs to God, you can be assured her heart belongs to you.

I know that when Scott makes suggestions or decisions that will affect the whole family, he seeks God's counsel. What about you? Can your wife trust that your heart belongs to God? When your wife can trust your heart, she will know that you desire God's will above all else. She'll be assured you are God-centered, not self-centered. When she is confident about these things, she'll respond more openly to you and your leadership because she feels secure and safe in your relationship.

The Master's Tools

I want to be honest. This journey of opening Carolina Courts has been difficult. Some days I cry, and on some days I tell God and my friends that it's too hard, that I can't do it. Some days I'm mad at Scott because of irrational feelings caused by fatigue, stress, and fear. Some days I start feeling resentful that he has shaken up our world with this big dream of his. On those days, I go to Jesus, and I pour out my heart to Him.

For a long time, I didn't understand Psalm 37:4: "Delight yourself in the LORD; and He will give you the desires of your heart." I used to approach this verse as if God were the Great Magic Fairy who would grant my wishes. I'd close my eyes and think something like this: *Lord, my desire is to have a secure income and plenty of money to live comfortably. I'd like healthy and happy children. And, of course, a marriage where my husband does what I think he should do.* Then I'd open my eyes and wait for God to perform His magic tricks. And I kept waiting and was sometimes quite put out that life was a bit more of a struggle than I expected, especially the marriage part.

Maybe you learned much more quickly than I did that God doesn't work like that. He's not a magic fairy. He loves each of us so much that He sent His precious Son to us to show how much He loves us and how He wants us to live. To refer back to the verse that used to baffle me, I've learned that something happens to your heart when you truly seek God first. When you go to God honestly and transparently, you begin to know God in a more intimate way. And as you know Him, you fall in love with Him, so much so that your heart's desire becomes God's heart's desire. More than anything, you begin to want to live the life He wants for you. That becomes your greatest desire.

So on those days when I'm ready to kick my big-dreaming, entrepreneurial husband out the door, I try to remember that this whole gym thing is not really about the gym thing. It's really about the journey of knowing our Lord and each other in a new, deeper way.

I've heard that the great Michelangelo was asked how he could look at a huge piece of marble and have the vision to see the statue of David. He replied, "I chipped away at the parts that weren't David." God does the same thing in each of our lives. Using a variety of tools, He chips away at the parts of our lives that are not who He created us to be. Over and over again as I write this book and reflect on my own marriage, I see that the number one tool God has used to develop my character and mature my faith has been my marriage. As we close this chapter about seeking God first, I pray that you will take time right now to seek God first, to delight in Him, and to reflect on how God has used your marriage as a tool in your own life.

PRAYER GUIDE

Heavenly Father,

Thank You for loving me and desiring a relationship with me, not a religion. Help me to hunger and thirst for You, and as I do, Lord, turn my heart in the directions that please You. Give me wisdom and the will to order my priorities and find a balance that is pleasing to You. Show me where I need to make changes in the way I spend my time, energy, and money, and let me be willing to confess this as sin and to make the changes You desire. Let my upmost desire be for You and to know You. Lord, I want to lead my family in a way that honors You. Let me be the one who leads our family in all matters, especially spiritual ones. I confess my fears and insecurities about being the spiritual leader and confess my failure in this area.

Finally, Lord, will You help me find other godly men, so we can encourage and support one another? Help me to open up to at least one other man. And help me to be open to the tools, especially the tool of my marriage, that You use in my life to shape me and mold me into the man You want me to be. Amen.

3

Love Her No Matter What

I clearly remember the details of my first date with Scott years ago in Atlanta. One particular detail, however, stands out to me. I found out several months later that the night before our first date, Scott had taken a "trial run" to my apartment. Driving to my place and back assured him he could find his way and would not be late to pick me up. He didn't reveal this until we'd been dating awhile, and when he did tell me, it opened up my heart to him.

Does this seem like an unlikely detail to become the highlight of our first date? Here's why it meant so much to me. It communicated so much to me about the way Scott might love me. His trial run seemed to say, *I've thought about you, and I want this date to be just right.* Scott invested extra time and energy into our first date, efforts which said to me, *You are important; you really matter to me.* His careful planning of this date foreshadowed the way he might continue to love me in the future.

What's Love Got to Do with It?

As I write this chapter, I can't help but think of the song "What's Love Got to Do with It?" Here's the answer from a woman's perspective: everything! Love matters enormously to your wife, and love matters more than anything to God. After all, God inspired the apostle Paul to write, "The greatest of these is love" (1 Corinthians 13:13).

God designed marriage, and He knows each spouse's needs. Both a husband and a wife need to feel loved, but love is one of the most significant needs for a wife. Love is what guides your wife, stabilizes her, assures her, and motivates her in your marriage.

Let's start by looking specifically at what the apostle Paul says to husbands about loving their wives. In Ephesians 5:25, Paul specifically addresses husbands. The Message paraphrase gets right to the point: "Husbands, go all out in your love for your wives, exactly as Christ did for the church—a love marked by giving, not getting." Paul tells husbands how to love their wives: "Go all out."

What will all-out love look like in your own marriage? You might think of grand gestures for your wife, such as taking her on a big trip or buying expensive jewelry. Extravagant expressions like these certainly may be appropriate on rare occasions, but that's not really what Paul was referring to. Here's some great news about going all out in your love for your wife: First and foremost, God wants you to love by going all out in your heart. That explains why the smallest acts, such as a sweet phone call or handwritten note, can make your wife feel loved enormously.

Speak Her Love Language

Most men I know would readily think, *I do love my wife! I'm going all out in my love for her by working hard each day to provide for her and the kids. I even saved up and took her on a cruise last year.* You might even think, *I married her, didn't I? Doesn't that prove I love her?*

If you are a hardworking man, I applaud you. Being the primary provider for a household is an enormous responsibility. You work diligently for her and the rest of your family, so you might think your love for her is obvious. But the key question is, does she *feel* loved? The things that actually make your wife feel loved might be very different from the things that make you feel loved or the things that you think should make her feel loved.

I believe most men have good intentions of wanting their wives to feel loved, but sometimes they're just puzzled about what will actually work. If you're not sure what to do, here are some guidelines.

- Pray for God to give you eyes to see what makes your wife feel loved. Remember throughout your journey as a husband that God is for your marriage and ready to help you.

- Ask your wife what makes her feel loved. If she's like me, she's eager to tell you!

- Observe her and listen to her to know how best to love her. Be a student of your wife.

- Be willing to do it. That's something God can help you with. Remind yourself that as you love your wife, you're really loving the Lord. "Whatever you do in word or deed, do all in the name of the Lord Jesus, giving thanks through Him to God the Father" (Colossians 3:17).

Scott and I have learned a lot about how to meet each other's need for love by reading Gary Chapman's book *The Five Love Languages*. It has helped us to love one another in the unique way we each need to be loved. Chapman explains that each of us has a need to be loved—we each come with a love tank needing to be filled. The five love languages are the various ways that love tank gets filled. They include words of affirmation, quality time, receiving gifts, acts of service, and physical touch.

We each have a primary love language that will make our love tanks full. Almost always, spouses have different love languages. We tend to express love the way we like to be loved. For example, if your love language is words of affirmation, that's how you'll love your spouse. You may not be filling up her love tank, however, if that's not her primary love language. My primary love language, for example, is quality time. When Scott is home and we eat dinner together, watch the kids play basketball, or take the dogs for a walk together, I feel loved. He can say all the sweet things in the world, and I do appreciate those sweet words (and as Scott likes to tease me, my love language seems to be all five), but I feel most loved through quality time together.

But Scott is different from me. Words of affirmation are his primary love language. Because this isn't my love language, I have to work hard to remember to praise him and verbally express my appreciation for him. When I do, however, the difference in him is easy to see. He is more motivated to love me—more motivated about everything! His tank is filled up, and he's energized.

Speaking your spouse's love language will often require sacrificial love. Gary Chapman explains his own experience in sacrificial love:

> My wife's love language is "Acts of Service." One of the things I do for her regularly as an act of love is to vacuum the floors. Do you think that vacuuming floors comes naturally for me? My mother used to make me vacuum. All through junior and senior high school, I couldn't go play ball on Saturday until I finished vacuuming the entire house. In those days, I said to myself, "When I get out of here, one thing I am not going to do: I am not going to vacuum houses. I'll get myself a wife to do that."
>
> But I vacuum our house now, and I vacuum it regularly. And there is only one reason I vacuum our house. *Love.* You couldn't pay me enough to vacuum a house, but I do it for love. You see, when an action doesn't come naturally to you, it is a greater expression of love. My wife knows that when I vacuum the house, it's nothing but 100 percent pure, unadulterated love, and I get credit for the whole thing! [1]

If you'll start speaking your wife's love language, she'll be much more likely to feel loved. Here are some ideas to get you started.

If her primary love language is words of affirmation, she may smile and light up when you praise her. Be sure to compliment her directly and to praise her to other people when she can hear. "I sure appreciate the way you keep this house running smoothly," "I'm so glad I'm married to you," and "I love you" will keep her heart soaring.

If her love language is quality time, make sure you're with her physically and emotionally. Consider your work schedule and how you might be home early enough to share in some family time. Take 15 minutes when you get home to listen to her with your undivided attention. Take her on a date.

If her love language is gifts, give her just about anything. The gifts do not have to be big or expensive. Try a gift of a card, a flower, her favorite snack, or anything else she's talked about and you remember to get for her.

If her love language is acts of service, do something for her. Her heart will open up when you clean out the garage, load the dishwasher, play with the kids, pick up that item she forgot at the grocery, or change a diaper.

If her love language is physical touch, make sure you hug her, hold hands, put your arm around her, and make love to her.

As I look over what I've written here, the truth is that all of these sound good to me! Your wife's love language will probably change somewhat with the seasons and stresses of marriage. Remember to always go back to the Lord and ask Him to show you how to best love your wife.

Show Her You Love Her

Your wife wants to hear the words "I love you," and then she wants you to back up those words with your actions. "Show me the money" became a catchphrase in our culture as a result of the popular movie *Jerry Maguire.* Tom Cruise played a character who repeated the phrase over and over. I can't help but think a wife's refrain might be, "Show me the love." That's how she'll know you're sincere. No one person could ever meet all of another person's needs, but in marriage, God wants a husband to partner with Him in loving his wife for Christ.

In this chapter we'll look at several ways your actions can show your wife you love her. Your wife feels loved when you make her feel like a top priority, help her, romance her, and love her at times when she feels unlovable.

Your Wife Feels Loved When She's Your Top Priority

When you and your wife were first dating, she found great satisfaction knowing that you chose her and then continued to woo and romance her. As she saw you making her a top priority in your life, she felt loved. You were trying to win her heart, and you knew she needed to see how much she mattered to you. For example, when Scott made his trial run to my apartment before our first date, he demonstrated to me that he was willing to go all out for me, and he continued to prove this during our courtship.

Now that you're married, your wife still needs to feel like your top priority. Men tend to go all out in their pursuit during dating and even into the first few years of marriage. Unfortunately, however, after a few years, many men tend to stop investing in the relationship. They seem to have checked off the marriage box, and now they're on to the next item on the list, perhaps pursuing something else such as a career or a hobby. One of the best ways to help your wife feel loved is to let her know again and again that you choose her. The marriage box is never permanently checked off her list, so don't check it off yours.

How do you make her feel like a top priority? Small gestures of thoughtfulness can make a big difference. A few weeks ago, Scott called me to say, "Sometimes it just hits me again how lucky I am to have you as my wife." This was in the midst of a very busy season when we seemed to go for days without having even a five-minute conversation.

That phone call said to me, *I know I've been super busy and stressed, but you're still the most important person in my life.*

A huge way to make your wife know she's your top priority is to give her your time. I've heard women say they feel as if they are competing with their husband's work or hobby for his attention. If your wife feels you are choosing those activities before her, she might shut down emotionally and withdraw. When her heart is hurting, she is not going to open it up to you only to be hurt again.

Another typical response to a lack of attention is anger. Roots of bitterness will grow deeper and deeper until you once again begin to convince her that you choose her first. When you get married, your time is no longer your own. You are not entitled to do what you want to do whenever you want to. That's one of the changes you must make to honor the oneness of your marriage.

Remember that the marriage God wants you to have starts with a change of heart. The surrendering of your marriage can often be in fits and starts. I lay my marriage at Christ's feet, surrendering my rights for His sake and for the sake of the marriage. But when I'm not happy with the way things are going in our relationship, I grab my marriage back from the altar and hold it tightly in my own grip. If you too have done that, go back to the Lord, confess your sin, and lay it down again.

Scott is an all-or-nothing kind of guy with many passions, dreams, and interests. Earlier in our marriage I felt as if his job, his hobbies, and our boys were more important to him than I was. Scott was not the only one contributing to our problems in this area. I was overly sensitive and tried to manipulate him into giving me the attention I wanted.

We had some sin to deal with. This pattern of Scott being busy and me being hurt and angry about it was well ingrained in our lives. The Bible calls our sinful, reflexive patterns of behavior "the flesh" or "the sinful nature" or "the old man." I encourage you to take some time to pray for God to reveal your flesh patterns so you can confess your sins, experience cleansing, and replace your old and harmful habits with new and helpful ways of living. This is not an easy process, but I can say from experience that it leads to freedom in Christ. You'll be free to be the man God wants you to be, released from slavery to your old sinful nature. Christ's death on a cross established our freedom, and now we learn how to live out that freedom as we mature in our relationship with Christ.

Nothing was wrong with me wanting to have the proper place in Scott's life. Likewise, nothing is wrong with the way Scott thrives on activity. We just had to deal with our sin so we could clear the way to a healthy balance of activities. We had to determine a way to make our personalities work together to enhance the oneness in our marriage. This was part of our journey in learning how to value "we" more than "me." As we learned to walk in the Spirit rather than the flesh, we grew in our maturity, and the oneness of our marriage increased.

Balancing life according to God's desires and design is a challenge for all of us, but God can help you make changes. I've seen Scott become much more balanced and willing to make changes. I've seen him choose family time over softball games, and I've seen him walk away from the computer even though he still had a lot of work to do. Just yesterday he built a gingerbread house with Tyler. He went to the store with Tyler and his buddy Mitchell, let them pick out all sorts of goodies, came home and made homemade frosting (he didn't even use the canned frosting), and spent several hours creating a gingerbread house. With our brand-new business, I know Scott had to choose to take the time to do that, and I know that choice was a sacrifice. The rewards, however, are huge. He has a close relationship with both our sons because he frequently makes choices like this one. Also, he knew this would free up some writing time for me. Yesterday, I felt enormously loved.

Your Wife Feels Loved When You Help Her

Most men I know will not ask for directions. They'll consult the GPS or the atlas, but asking another human being for directions is apparently against the rules. I know that's a generalization, so just to be fair, I'll make one about women: Women ask, and they liked to be asked. In fact, one way to make your wife feel loved is to ask her what she needs from you. Specifically ask her, "What can I do to help you?" Every woman I know is a multitasker. This is the way God designed us, and this characteristic is actually a beautiful gift from God. A woman can encourage a friend on the phone, read a new recipe, answer her child's question, and feed the dog—all at the same time. She does this all well and sincerely while giving appropriate responses and attention.

Even though multitasking is a gift, it also can wear a woman out as she has a constant to-do list running through her head. In addition, these activities are loaded with emotions: *I hope Zach has a good practice because he didn't last time and he was so discouraged. I hope my sister's getting some rest because she's been so stressed-out. I miss Scott and wish he didn't have to work out of town this week.* Women can wear themselves out with all these thoughts! So when a husband offers to help, he eases her load, just as we're told to do in Galatians 6:2: "Bear one another's burdens, and thereby fulfill the law of Christ."

I have a little mental list of my top five needs. This is my "Things You Can Do for Me Anytime" list:

- Without being asked, do any household chore I normally do.
- Do anything with our two sons.
- Massage my shoulders and neck.
- Say, "I appreciate you."
- Bring me a small gift, such as my favorite Harris Teeter chocolate chip cookies

Whenever Scott performs any one of these, I feel loved. Why don't you ask your wife right now to create a list for you? That way you don't always have to ask, and when you're not sure what to do, you'll have some pretty good ideas. Of course, your wife reserves the right to change this list at any time!

As you use this list, you'll begin to anticipate her needs without being asked, and this will meet her needs even more effectively. Wendy Pope, director of development for Proverbs 31 Ministries, tells about a time her husband showed his love by anticipating her needs:

> My husband is a student of me—my habits, likes, dislikes, schedule, and anything else that has to do with me. I was completely unaware of his studies, but recently his actions spoke loud and clear of what he had been doing.
>
> My morning schedule is very important to me. I get up just in time to do all the things I need to do in order to get our children and myself out the door on time. One morning, I overslept by only ten minutes, but to a woman, ten minutes is crucial to a schedule.
>
> I was scurrying around to get myself ready: shower, dress, makeup, and hair. As I walked by the bed, I noticed my husband was not there. I made my way to the kitchen, mentally preparing for the next task, only to find him doing it: making breakfast.
>
> My anxious heart began to slow down as I released a huge sigh and a southern "Awww." I had no idea my husband had been studying the clock while I was preparing for our family's day. This particular morning, he looked at the clock, knew what I normally did at that time, and realized I was running behind. He also knew that being late makes me anxious and yes, cranky. He gave himself up for me by leaving a warm bed in the dark of the early morning to demonstrate his love for me.

Wendy's story reminds us again of Ephesians 5:25: "Husbands, love your wives, just as Christ also loved the church and gave Himself up for her." So with what kind of love did Christ love the church?

Sacrificial love. That's the kind of love a husband needs to show his wife. A love that doesn't consider his own needs first.

Your Wife Feels Loved When You Romance Her

When we are first married, we are so full of love we hardly have to think about how to romance our spouses. We're just overwhelmed with the wonder of marriage. Life is like the best birthday ever, and your spouse is the best present you could imagine. But soon, like a forgotten present, a bright and shiny marriage can get tarnished and dented as you deal with everyday responsibilities, raise children, pursue careers, manage finances, struggle with a crisis, and live with someone who is probably very different from you just because she's the opposite sex. If you find yourself feeling a little tarnished, it may be time to romance your wife. Romancing your wife will help you both celebrate the shiny gift of marriage. Romance carries you and your wife beyond the everyday routine of life.

Romance grows out of the little touches. It includes being considerate when you open her car door, delicate when you hold her hand or put your arm around her. Romance is thoughtful when you ask about a difficult situation at her job, reassuring when you hug her tightly. Romance is heartfelt when you say "I love you" every day.

Romance can be creative, spontaneous, and unexpected. One friend secretly arranged to take his wife on an island cruise. After getting the kids settled with her parents, he packed their bags, and she didn't find out where they were going till they got the tickets. Another friend arranged a citywide scavenger hunt. She went from store to store, gathering clues that led to a hotel where her husband was waiting, and they spent a night away.

During our wedding ceremony 18 years ago, our pastor instructed us to always date one another. At the time I thought, *Of course we'll date each other.* Before long, however, I realized how easily dates can be moved down the list of priorities. Taking your wife on a date is romantic to her. If you initiate the date, set aside the time one night, and even make the babysitter arrangements, that's super-romantic! Think about what kind of date she likes. Some women like creativity and variety. If so, surprise her by taking her to a new place. Other women are like me—they like tradition. I love to go to my favorite restaurant in Waxhaw, North Carolina—Rippington's—for dinner. Follow that with a movie, and I'm a happy wife!

Romance reminds you both that once upon a time you chose your wife, and you'd choose her again. Ingrained in your wife is a need to know that you find her beautiful, that you don't notice the 15 pounds she gained and never lost through the years, that you don't mind the laugh lines around her eyes. She wants to wear something pretty, spend extra time on her hair, complete it with lipstick, and be admired. She wants to be the object of your affection and attention.

You might feel somewhat out of your comfort zone being romantic. Remember those stiff Wrangler jeans I described in the first chapter? They get comfortable only as you wear them, just like the new habits you're practicing in your marriage.

Here's a word of caution: Don't romance your wife to get what you want. Romance her because you love her and because she needs you to. When she sees you're not trying to get something from her, she'll feel cherished and fall a little more in love once again.

As the years pass, the feelings of romance commonly wane. That's okay. Sometimes we mistakenly assume that because we don't have those intensely passionate moments as frequently as we did while dating, our love has diminished. Don't fall into this trap. The years of marriage allow you to explore other types of love too, and those types of love are just as important.

Love Her as Only a Husband Can

When I was pregnant with our second son, Tyler, I was not at my best. Actually, I was a mess. We lived in Palm Beach Gardens, Florida, at the time, a lovely but really hot place for a pregnant lady. I was hot all the time and cranked our air conditioner down so low that condensation formed on the windows. I was huge and uncomfortable. Tyler ended up being a big baby—9 pounds, 15 ounces—but that doesn't justify the other 40 pounds I gained.

I was hungry all the time but easily nauseated, so cooking anything involving raw meat was not an option. I was also tired, so after teaching and getting little Zachary tucked in early, I was done for the day. When trying to go to sleep, I soon became very sensitive to any outside noises, so we nailed several blankets over our windows, attempting to muffle the noise.

I pity Scott for having to live with me during that pregnancy. Amazingly, he loved me with kindness, patience, and longsuffering. Although we joke now that he earned many jewels in his heavenly crown during that pregnancy, I needed to be sure of his love during that time.

That's a kind of love that only a husband can give. A love that sees the good, the bad, and the ugly and still says, *I love you now, and I'll always love you.* I am sure Scott thought then and has thought many times since that he married a crazy lady, but he has loved me unconditionally.

A Christian marriage reflects God's love, a covenant love. God's covenant love does not depend on anything we do or don't do. God's love just is. In the same way, a Christian couple demonstrates this covenant love as they remain committed to each other during hard times. Their commitment does not depend on pleasant circumstances. In other words, their love is not conditional, as so many marriages in today's world are. A covenant love promises, "till death do us part," and perseveres in the hard times.

The Dangers of Not Making Your Wife Feel Loved

Because feeling loved is one of a woman's top needs, she is constantly taking the temperature of the relationship. Even if she's not totally aware that she's doing this, she is looking for assurance of your love. That's why a seemingly insignificant slight, such as not kissing her goodbye, can escalate quickly to her accusing you of not loving her.

When your wife feels unloved, your marriage is exposed to several dangers. Some of the flesh patterns I mentioned above will creep into her heart and camp out in your marriage like unwelcome guests. Some of the most common intruders for women are unforgiveness, bitterness, coldheartedness, jealousy, fear, and insecurity.

You might not have thought about another intruder that you need to be aware of—Satan. He caused havoc in the very first marriage between Adam and Eve, and marriage continues to be his battleground. If he sees even the smallest crack in the door of marriage, he will barge right in, hunker down, and try to take up residence. Once he gets in, getting him back out is difficult. The best plan of attack is to never let him in. Slam the door in his face by praying, inviting God to use all His power to fight for your marriage, and practicing the godly principles that help you to be the kind of husband God wants you to be.

This chapter has many ideas you can put into practice right now in your marriage. I hope you'll try many of them, and I hope you'll find your marriage enriched as you do. Here's a warning: At some point, you're going to love your wife the way you think she needs or wants you to, but you won't get the response you were expecting or hoping for. Don't get discouraged or give up. That's what the enemy would want. He wants to turn you and your wife against each other, to make you think your wife is the enemy. Don't let him have any victory or even get a foothold in your marriage. Continue loving your wife because that's what God wants you to do. You are the one God chose to love your wife.

The Gift of a Good Relationship

When people think of Mark and Cindy, they immediately say things like, "Mark just adores Cindy," or "They have an incredible marriage." I asked Cindy to tell me about their relationship so we could have a glimpse into what makes their marriage so strong.

Our good relationship is God's gift in our lives. It isn't just a tribute to us. I think God gave it to us as a gift. That's how we shine for Him—through our marriage. We have so many other areas we fail in, so I can speak freely about our marriage without feeling like I'm boasting. The one area that truly is a blessing and weathers every single storm is our marriage.

In a nutshell, Mark loves me by always putting me first—before his own feelings, before his own agenda, and before his own comfort. We've had some challenges recently—nine months of unemployment and trials with our son. Even during this trying season of our marriage, I see how much of a servant Mark is to me. He serves freely and from his heart. He'll be the first one to see what I need—he'll encourage me to take a nap if he sees I'm tired. He'll have dinner ready for me or make an appetizer and just sit and talk with me. He puts me first. He loves loving me.

Last night I couldn't sleep. I'm hesitant to wake him up in the middle of the night, although he does tell me to. I don't think very many husbands would tell their wives to wake them up. They want their own comfort, their own sleep, and I understand because I'm more like that. But last night I did wake Mark up. He did what he usually does. He rubbed my feet because he knows that relaxes me. He just let me talk, and he listened. I'm blessed to have a husband who thinks what I say is interesting and important. He holds my opinions highly. He makes me feel important.

I can't imagine ever having another Mark. No one else could love me the way he loves me.

Two things stood out to me when talking to Cindy. First, she said, "That's how we shine for Him—through our marriage." Second, she said what every wife would like to say: "He loves loving me."

PRAYER GUIDE

Dear Lord,

Thank You for choosing me to love my wife for You. I want to go all out in my love for my wife, just the way You do in Your love for me. Help me be Your heart, hands, and feet in our marriage. I know I can do that only as You pour Your love through me. I cannot do that in my own strength. Lord, if any sin is an obstacle in our marriage, reveal that to me. Thank You for forgiving me and turning my heart toward my wife in love. Put a hedge of protection around our marriage and protect us from the attacks of the enemy. Lord, let me love my wife the way she needs to be loved and the way You want me to love her. Amen.

4

He Said, She Said

A recent conversation with my husband went something like this:

"Scott, I want to finish up Christmas shopping this week, so can we talk about the boys' presents?"

"Uh-huh."

"I've already told them this will be a smaller Christmas as far as presents and that the relatives won't be sending as much as they normally do. You know, I thought I'd be okay not being with any family this Christmas, but I am really missing everyone. I wish we could hop on a plane and see everyone, but I know we can't. Mom and Dad are going to New York City. You know, we've always said we were going to take Tyler to New York City. Maybe we can do that next year after we see how things are going at the gym. I drove by the gym the other day and it looks like they've completed the parking lot."

About this time I noticed Scott had the "deer in the headlights" look. It's familiar to most men. It's an expression that communicates, *What's the point of this conversation, and can we end it soon?* If Scott could have written the script for the same conversation, it might sound something like this:

> Melanie: "I'm going to order some Timberwolves clothes for Zachary for Christmas and Lego sets for Tyler. Does that sound good to you?"
>
> Scott: "Sure."
>
> Melanie: "Okay."

Better yet...

> Melanie: "Do you care what I get the boys for Christmas?"
>
> Scott: "No."
>
> Melanie: "Okay."

As you can see from this conversation (and countless conversations you've had with your wife), men and women communicate differently. The challenge in marriage is to learn to communicate in a way that enhances intimacy and oneness instead of obscuring it with miscommunication. Good communication is vital to your marriage. In fact, studies show that more than 80 percent of divorced couples name poor communication as the main cause of their split.

God wants you to experience the greatest intimacy possible with Him and with your wife. Genesis 2:24-25 confirms that God wants you to be closer to your wife than to any other human being: "For this reason a man shall leave his father and his mother, and be joined to his wife; and they shall become one flesh. And the man and his wife were both naked and were not ashamed." The words "naked and were not ashamed" give us a picture of not only physical intimacy but also emotional intimacy. One of the ways to foster this is to develop good communication.

Her Number One Need: For You to Listen and Talk

When I asked women what they need from their husbands, their number one answer was that they need their husbands to communicate. Learning to talk and listen in a way that meets your wife's needs is crucial to building a strong marriage. Jenny explains how listening meets her needs: "Listening helps me to feel validated; listening helps me to feel important; listening helps me to feel connected; listening helps me to feel cherished."

As I've been writing and speaking about marriage over the past few years, I've discovered how lonely many women feel. One woman said to me, "I just wish I had a husband who would talk to me. I never know what he's thinking or feeling." God never intended for a spouse to feel lonely or alone in marriage. God's plan is just the opposite. In fact, God is the one who said it was not good for Adam to be alone. So He gave him Eve, a companion to share the journey of life, so neither of them would be lonely. In the same way, your wife needs you to share life with, and one of the main ways she wants to do that is through communication.

The book of Proverbs tells us so much about talking. Proverbs 18:21 is a key verse to apply to communication in your marriage: "The tongue can bring death or life; those who love to talk will reap the consequences" (NLT). Clearly, good communication is critical for keeping your marriage emotionally alive and thriving. On the other hand, the wrong kind of words and communication can undermine a marriage and move a couple toward isolation. In this chapter you'll learn some practical ways to engage your wife in good communication.

Enjoy the Journey

A wife needs to feel emotionally connected to her husband through talking. This is how she best expresses her true self. So think about what you communicate to your wife if you don't talk. You're essentially telling her you don't want to know her.

I have sometimes felt hurt when Scott didn't communicate with me, so I withdrew from him. I gave him short answers, I didn't ask him how he was doing, and I didn't look for ways to serve him. I interacted with him as little as possible. Eventually, Scott usually asked me if something was bothering me. I remained cold and aloof by answering, "It doesn't matter. You won't really listen anyway." Yes, I know this is sinful behavior on my part, and in no way am I holding this behavior up as a positive example. However, I share this to show you how a wife might respond if her husband hasn't taken the time to talk and to listen—in other words, to emotionally connect.

One of the reasons couples may find communication difficult is that men and women communicate differently. For a woman, one idea leads to another, and they're all logically connected in her mind, as you noticed in the conversation between Scott and me at the beginning of the chapter. Of course, a man may feel as if his wife's thoughts are bouncing around like so many Ping Pong balls, and following them may be difficult for him.

Let me give you a way to picture your wife's way of thinking. Imagine a married couple on a road trip. The husband will not stop for anything—well, maybe one restroom stop, but that's it. He has a destination, and the goal is to get there as efficiently as possible. If he can beat a previous driving time, he will feel enormously satisfied. This is often how men approach conversations with their wives: They have a destination, and they need to get there as quickly as possible.

Your wife, on the other hand, approaches the road trip as if it's a journey, not merely a means to an end. She wants to enjoy the trip, savor the time together, and notice the interesting sites along the way. "Let's stop at that roadside stand because they probably have the best peaches around…We can't pass by that pottery store. They might have just the right Christmas present for your parents." In the same way, she's going to enjoy the journey of conversations with you by giving you details, including seemingly irrelevant and unrelated details. She's going to take her time and enjoy the journey.

Try to learn to enjoy the journey of conversations with your wife simply because she needs this from you. When Scripture tells us that we are created male and female, God is telling us to expect differences between our genders and to embrace the differences. If you resist this difference, you will miss out on the deep closeness God desires for you and your wife. When your wife says she wants to talk to you, she's not just asking for information. She is saying, "I want to be close with you, and talking is how I do that."

Your wife's approach to talking is different from yours, and her need to talk is probably greater than yours. Recognize that it's a need that is not going to go away. The need to connect through communication drives her. Think about one of your strongest needs, a need that drives you. If you're like many men, one of your driving needs is for sex. It's such a strong need that one husband said the solution to all this talking stuff would be just to have sex, and then he'd be willing to talk. I bet if you're willing to have more conversations, your wife will be willing to have more sex. Try it!

Consider Your Attitude

Four little words spoken by a wife can send fear into the heart of the bravest and strongest of men: "We need to talk." What do you think when your wife says this to you?

- *Oh no—I'm in the doghouse about something.*

- *The play-off game is starting in five minutes. I hope we can cut to the chase.*

- *Oh, for crying out loud! We talked about this yesterday—it's time to get over it.*

- *You bet! I love to talk! I can't wait to hear what you have to say.*

Seriously—take a moment to consider what you think about

your wife's desire to talk with you. Are you receptive or resistant? A negative attitude will be as obvious to her as the nose on your face. In this chapter you'll find some suggestions for being receptive to communication with your wife.

The difference between men's and women's approaches to communication can be a factor in a man's resistance to talking. Women connect; men compartmentalize. Bill and Pam Farrel explain this in their enlightening book *Men Are Like Waffles—Women Are Like Spaghetti.*

> Men process life in boxes. If you look down at a waffle, you see a collection of boxes separated by walls. The boxes are all separate from each other and make convenient holding places. That is typically how a man processes life. Our thinking is divided up into boxes that have room for one issue and one issue only. The first issue of life goes in the first box, the second goes in the second box, and so on. The typical man lives in one box at a time and one box only. When a man is at work, he is at work. When he is in the garage tinkering, he is in the garage tinkering. When he is watching TV, he is simply watching TV...
>
> In contrast to men's waffle-like approach, women process life more like a plate of pasta. If you look at a plate of spaghetti, you notice that there are lots of individual noodles that all touch one another. If you attempted to follow one noodle around the plate, you would intersect a lot of other noodles, and you might even switch to another noodle seamlessly. That is how women face life. Every thought and issue is connected to every other thought and issue in some way.[1]

Even as I write this, I'm laughing at the incredible truth to this. Sometimes we just have to laugh, or we'll find ourselves more ticked off than tickled. I can think of times when Scott was sitting in the home office working on his computer, and our son Tyler wandered in and said, "Dad. Dad. Dad." Getting no response at all from Scott, Tyler continued. "Dad. Dad. Dad." No response. As I'm working on my computer in the same room, I immediately hear Tyler because I'm a woman and women are tuned into everything simultaneously. I am absolutely confounded that Scott neither hears nor responds. After a minute of this I yell, "Scott! Tyler's talking to you!" Then Scott will turn and look at Tyler as if he never knew Tyler was there—and again, amazingly to me, he never did.

This isn't something to change but rather something to work with. Just make sure you create a box for communicating with your wife, and enter that box when she needs you to!

Communication Playbook

Scott and 14-year-old Zachary came home from watching a middle school team play basketball. As they discussed the performance of the other team, Zachary observed, "Dad, that team would be so much better if they talked to each other out on the court." I thought how true that is of a marriage team. We are not effective team members without communication. In this section you'll learn some practical ways to enhance communication. Many of these ideas have been gathered from couples who have reaped their rewards for several years in their marriage.

Establish a Face-to-Face Communication Ritual

Your wife needs to count on a face-to-face time to connect with you. This works best if it's a regular time and a daily ritual. Susan explains that she and Steve discovered the benefits of a talking ritual:

> When we moved to Alabama, we really struggled with communication. We had a third grader, a preschooler, and a four-month-old. I was fried, Steve was fried, and we both

were getting used to living in the deep South, which was very different from our East and West Coast living. We got into counseling, and the counselor recommended that at the end of the day, after the kids are in bed, we turn off the TV and spend 30 minutes face-to-face talking. So we began to make this a routine at the same time every night, and now, many years later, we still do it. Steve knows talking at the end of the day before we go to bed makes bedtime a lot more fun!

Technology Can Support Your Communication

Nothing can substitute for face-to-face communication, but you can definitely use electronic means of communication to stay in touch with your wife. Phone calls, e-mails, and texting help a wife feel connected to her husband.

Scott has traveled with his work as a pilot for 14 of our 18 years of marriage. He is great at calling me throughout the day, wherever he is. I feel a great deal of security knowing he's only a phone call away. I would feel shut out if I couldn't call him and count on being able to reach him. Even if he's in the air and can't answer the phone, he returns my call as soon as he can. I love knowing how important I am to him and knowing I'm on his mind, especially if he's been gone several days in a row.

E-mailing is another way to stay connected, as Kelly Bridgeforth says: "Sometimes I will e-mail my husband. That way he doesn't need to come up with an immediate response. This usually works pretty well because we get to express our feelings if we've been offended. It gives us time to cool off before responding."

Mandy and Butch exchange texts throughout the day. Mandy says, "If I know he's in a boring meeting, I can send him a funny, flirtatious, or sexy message to make his day a little more enjoyable. It lets him know I'm thinking about him even in the midst of my crazy day. Sometimes I even say things I might not have the nerve to say in person."

How to Listen

One need surfaces repeatedly as I talk to women about communication with their husbands. Women continually say, "I want my husband to realize that he doesn't have to fix the problem. I just need him to listen." Fixing problems is second nature to most men. It's what they're wired to do. This is a wonderful quality—if that's what your wife is looking for. Many times she will want you to simply listen first without problem solving. You may think you *do* listen, but if you move immediately toward fixing the problem and providing her a solution, she will not feel heard. The apostle James writes that being a good listener is crucial. "Everyone must be quick to hear, slow to speak and slow to anger" (James 1:19).

You might think you are a good listener, but the question is, does your wife think so? Listening and hearing are two different things, and your wife needs to feel heard. Counselor Dan Ascher suggests a communication technique that will help your wife to feel heard:

- Listen, engaging your mind and heart. Let her tell you her thoughts and feelings.
- Summarize what your wife said. Here's the key: When you summarize or rephrase, you must include not only the content of what she said but also the heart and feelings of what she said.
- Allow her to tell you whether you heard what she wanted you to hear.

Learning to communicate this way provides several advantages. You avoid assumptions, which can so often be erroneous, and you eliminate arguments that result from miscommunication. People often try to read each other's minds, but that usually isn't very effective.

This technique takes time and practice, but its soothing and calming effect on a woman is amazing. When a husband listens this way, he allows his wife to do something that's very important to her: process her thoughts and feelings aloud. A woman uses talking aloud to process life. Kim Sheley explains this so well: "Women like to talk, and really talk over things that are bothering them, and sometimes 'overtalk' a situation. Even when I can't quit dwelling on something, I need Dave just to listen."

Once you've listened, your wife may want your input, and she may even want you to help her come up with a solution. You can ask her, "Do you want to know what I think might work in this situation?" Kim continues to explain: "I need him to give me perspective and advice, to help me make the right decisions and let me bounce stuff off of him. I don't always take his advice, but by listening, he helps me to make the right decisions on most matters, even if the problems are very small and silly."

Support Her Emotionally

Today was one of those days when nothing seemed to go right and everything was a bigger deal than it really should have been. About halfway through the day, I called to vent and get some support from Scott. Yes, I was weepy and emotional, and I'm sure he was thinking, *What is up with that?* We were talking on cell phones, and our connection was breaking up, which added to my irritation, so I said, "Just forget it; I'll call you later." About half an hour later, Scott walked in the door, and I cried some more. Sensing I needed some TLC, he came home from work in the middle of the day just to be there for me. That made my bad day a lot better.

Your wife needs your emotional support. You don't have to understand completely, just as Scott didn't completely understand the cause of my emotions. Just be there for her. That's what will feel supportive to her. As Tracey says, "I need emotional support and patience. Even if I'm ranting about something that seems totally stupid and irrational, I want to know that he always has my back."

Body Language and Tone of Voice

Women are very relational and are tuned into everything around them. Consequently, your wife not only hears your words but also notices what you're saying with your body language. Just the other day Scott and I were having a "heated discussion." We knew we would soon be interrupted by the kids, the dogs, or the phone. I could sense him losing focus, which I interpreted as losing interest in what I had to say, so I made a preemptive move by yelling, "Don't even think about looking away!" You can imagine how well the rest of that conversation went!

Your wife wants your undivided attention. Catherine explains that one of the ways her husband, Ron, loves her is by giving her his attention. "When I walk in the room where he's watching TV, he immediately mutes the TV to ask if I want to talk to him. Or if he's reading the newspaper, I watch him purposefully put it down and look at me, and I know he's ready to talk to me. These little gestures make me feel loved, valued, and appreciated."

As your wife is talking, she is also searching your face, and she notices small nuances that signal to her that you're listening—or not. These examples of body language can help your communication:

> eye contact (This is a biggie!)
> leaning toward her
> nodding your head
> touching her

Women have told me quite a bit about body language that deters communication:

> interrupting
> rolling your eyes
> crossing your arms
> sighing or exhaling loudly, as if listening is exhausting
> finishing her sentences
> looking at the TV or computer

answering your cell phone

looking at your watch

turning your body away from her

allowing yourself to be distracted

Tone of Voice Speaks Volumes

Along with body language, your tone of voice can help or hinder communication. Does your wife ever say to you, "Stop yelling at me!"

And maybe you respond, "I'm not yelling. This is not yelling."

Then she says, "I'm not talking to you if you're going to yell at me." Your wife is sensitive not only to your words but also to the way you say them. If you raise your voice, your wife will probably feel as if you're yelling, and then she won't hear a thing you say. You can also short-circuit your communication by sounding harsh, critical, sarcastic, impatient, insensitive, abrupt, lecturing, demeaning, condescending, or demanding. Work on speaking to your wife with a kind, courteous, and gentle tone of voice.

Emotional Hunger

Do you ever stop by the grocery store on the way home from work? Maybe you need just one item, and you have every intention of just getting that one thing. But you're really hungry, and as you go down the aisles, the ice cream looks better than ever, the chips and salsa are calling your name, and somehow you end up with your cart filled with the most appealing but junkiest food you can imagine.

A similar thing happens to your wife when a lack of connection and communication in your marriage leaves her emotionally hungry. Junk food starts to look more appealing than a healthy meal. She goes to work, where she notices how friendly John is as he greets her each morning. He's thoughtful too, as he offers to get her a cup of coffee when he goes on a break. She goes to church Wednesday night and runs into Alan, a great guy you've known for years. Alan stops to greet her, and they end up talking quite a while. Later she thinks about the way Alan looked her right in the eyes when he was talking, and she remembers feeling as if he really cared about what she was saying. The conversation just flowed, and they could have talked a long time. For a moment she has a fleeting thought that it sure would be nice if she could talk as easily to her husband...

Your wife wants emotional closeness with you, but if she's not getting this connection with you, she will consciously or unconsciously find it elsewhere. Maybe she will have a network of friends who fill that void or a ministry or job that satisfies her. These are enriching and valuable connections, but they don't replace what she needs from you. Good communication is what makes her feel connected to you.

The most dangerous consequence of a woman feeling disconnected from her husband is that her thoughts and heart can become unguarded. She might find herself having thoughts about other men. She might compare you to these men and find herself longing for more than she is receiving from you. The junk food of another relationship will unexpectedly satisfy her hunger.

This is a dangerous path that could potentially lead to an affair. Most people don't plan to have affairs; they say things like "It just happened," though of course this is not really true. We simply must be purposeful about the choices we make. Do our choices facilitate oneness in our marriages or hinder it? An unguarded mind or heart can easily lead to an emotional or physical affair.

Be Your Wife's Friend

Although I can say today that Scott is my best friend, that hasn't always been the case. When we first were married, I was so close to my twin sister that Scott felt excluded when the three of us were together. Also, I had some very close girlfriends who, even in the first few years of my marriage, provided more emotional support than Scott did.

Gradually, however, we both learned to develop our friendship with one another. We reached a big turning point when we left Atlanta, where I had been single and then newly married, and moved to Florida for Scott's new flying job. Living in a new city where we knew few other people, we learned to depend on each other for friendship in a way we hadn't learned before.

Scott now is the one I turn to first just to be my friend, not in the way a girlfriend is a friend, but in a way that only a husband can be. The support that this kind of friendship brings is reflected in Ecclesiastes 4:9: "Two are better than one."

God's Word says we'll reap what we sow (Galatians 6:7), and we'd be wise to realize that the seeds of friendship and emotional intimacy we plant today will continue to bloom later in our marriages. We've all seen older couples sitting at restaurant tables, eating their entire meal in complete silence—no tender smiles, no small touches of care, no gazing into one another's eyes. Someday the kids will be gone, we will retire from our jobs, and the dust will settle. Then we will either enjoy one another's friendship or experience the loneliness of living with a stranger.

I don't want to look like those silent couples, and I'm sure you don't either. I want to grow old relishing my friendship with my husband, a friendship forged over years of sharing life's big and small moments.

Take time to develop a close friendship with your wife. Your wife wants to be close to you, not to someone else. She's looking for a full-course meal in your relationship, not just an appetizer. Let's look at some ways good communication can help to develop that friendship.

1. Ask about her interests. What's going on at your wife's job? If she talks about a stressful project or a boring meeting, take note. Follow up by asking for more details. She will appreciate your thoughtfulness. What are her hobbies or other interests? Does she scrapbook, serve in a ministry, write, blog, go to the gym, or go to a Bible study? One wife told me, "I want my husband to be interested in me and my life. I want him to ask about my blog and read it, to ask about my ministry and support it with prayer and concern, and to ask about my creative projects and show genuine interest in them."

2. Share an interest. What do you both like to do? Can you start doing something together? Our friends Tracey and Ron take short trips to the mountains, which is more Tracey's passion than Ron's, but he's learned to enjoy it too. My mom and dad have shared a love of travel over the years. They're also great cooks and have created some incredible meals together. Sharing time together with the bond of a common interest strengthens the friendship in your marriage. If you don't already have a shared hobby or pastime, start trying out some activities.

3. Encourage her. I've heard encouragement described as "putting courage in someone." Scott has done that for me. I started writing professionally in my late thirties, and before that, I had never considered this path. As more and more writing opportunities opened up, Scott encouraged me to go for it. If I ask him to read something and give me feedback, he makes time and gives me his honest opinion in an affirming way. His words are like fuel in my tank when I'm tired or experiencing a difficult writing day.

Encourage your wife with words like these: "You are so organized. Thank you for all the details you handle for our family." "Our kids are so lucky to have you as their mother." Most women have memories like elephants when it comes to their husbands' comments, regardless of whether they're positive or negative. Give your wife words of life, words she can hang on to during her day, words that will keep her motivated to do what God has called her to do. Your words of encouragement and praise lift her beyond herself and beyond her circumstances. They remind her of who she is in your eyes and in God's eyes.

4. Be careful with your words about her. Be careful how you talk to others about your wife. A good test is to remember that Jesus hears what you're saying about your wife. Would you say this in front of

Jesus? Would you say it in front of your wife? Let your words about her be kind, positive, and affirming. Also, make sure that your words don't violate her privacy and that they present her in the best possible light. Don't bad-mouth her to your family, friends, or coworkers. I love this word picture: "Watch the way you talk. Let nothing foul or dirty come out of your mouth. Say only what helps, each word a gift" (Ephesians 4:29 MSG). The phrase "each word a gift" is a great visual. Picture your words as beautifully wrapped presents you can give your wife, even if she's not around to hear them.

Handling Conflict in a Healthy Way

You want to spend your bonus money on a big-screen TV; she wants to update the furniture in the family room. You like the radio on in the car; she likes it off. Your idea of a good vacation is a weekend in the mountains; she'd rather go to the beach. From small irritations to bigger, more emotionally charged disagreements, a married couple is going to experience some kind of conflict throughout their years together. The key is not to avoid conflict altogether, but to handle it in a healthy way.

I can seem like the most easygoing person to everyone else, but when it comes to arguments with Scott, I become highly emotional in the blink of an eye. James 4:1 goes to the heart of this: "What is the source of quarrels and conflicts among you? Is not the source your pleasures that wage war in your members? You lust and do not have; so you commit murder. You are envious and cannot obtain; so you fight and quarrel." We can feel angry or hurt in conflicts with our spouses, but if we take time to look at the sources of these feelings, we see that "we lust and do not have." In other words, we want something that we're not getting. Often I want Scott to admit I'm right, to see things my way, to agree to my course of action. When I get focused on these things, we probably won't have a good conversation. What are some guidelines for the inevitable conflicts in marriage?

1. Seek harmony. In a conflict, both husband and wife must learn to focus on harmony. What's going to be best for your marriage? Sometimes I need to ask myself, is this really important in the long run? Or do I just want to get my way? So many issues become nonissues when I look at them from this perspective. Also, sometimes we can't seem to reach an agreement. In those times, we just have to agree to disagree. And of course, husbands and wives constantly have opportunities to compromise—we'll go to my family's for Thanksgiving and his for Christmas, and next year we'll switch.

2. Listen for facts and also for emotions. Earlier in this chapter I explained that your wife feels heard when you've listened not only to the facts but also to her heart. Especially in a disagreement, your wife will often express an underlying emotion, but neither of you will immediately realize what that emotion is. Women often experience a hidden fear, worry, or concern. For example, if your wife says to you, "I really wish you would take more time at night to read with Patrick," she could be expressing several things that are important to her. She undoubtedly thinks it's important for you to spend quality time with your son. She might be worried about your child's reading. She could be worn-out from being the one who usually does the reading at night and secretly hoping to transfer that responsibility to you. Taking time to hear your wife's heart facilitates understanding and closeness.

3. Identify your ungodly patterns. God's Word tells us that He wants us to be peacemakers, and Jesus Himself is named the Prince of Peace. But we will not find peace if we are walking in the flesh and not the Spirit. Nothing reveals our flesh patterns as clearly as our responses when we are angry or hurt. As we saw earlier, flesh patterns are those ingrained habits and behaviors we learned before becoming new creations in Christ.

Recognizing your flesh patterns during conflict can help you turn from them and develop new patterns of behavior that enable you to handle conflict in a healthy manner. You have to be honest with yourself and with the Lord about your flesh pattern, confess it as sin, and replace it with the new pattern of behavior as Christ empowers you. You become a new creation in Christ day by day as you practice God's ways rather than sinful ways. Common fleshly responses to anger include defensiveness, offensiveness, blaming, attacking, being overly emotional, being overly logical, name-calling, sarcasm, and withdrawal. These patterns often surface in the heat of a conflict, but God will enable you to change. You can handle even a highly charged fight in a godly manner.

4. *Make some words off-limits.* In a heated argument, attacking one another with hurtful words is all too easy. To prevent this, establish some rules up front about words you will never say to one another. One wife told her husband at the beginning of their marriage never to say she's acting like her mother. One word that married couples should never say is *divorce,* or any words that imply the same thing, such as "I was crazy to ever marry you." Don't even go there. God's Word is clear in Malachi 2:16 that God hates divorce. If you find yourself even thinking about divorce, let alone talking about it, this should be a huge red flag that you have some deep issues to address with God, each other, and a Christian counselor.

5. *Silence doesn't work.* Some husbands are so averse to conflict that they may respond to tension in a way that completely frustrates their wives: They become silent. The most frustrating thing a husband can do in a conflict or when his wife needs to talk to him is to retreat or withdraw. When I think about a husband who withdraws from his wife, I picture a turtle tucking in his head and limbs.

As I was studying what Scripture says about words, I came across a verse that aptly speaks to this situation of withdrawal: "He who separates himself seeks his own desire" (Proverbs 18:1). Often a husband withdraws from a situation because he doesn't want to engage with his wife. He just wants to do what he wants to do, and he certainly doesn't want to hear any objections from her. In fact, some husbands withdraw from their wives intentionally. They know their wives want to talk, so being silent is one way they can gain the upper hand and feel in control.

6. Allow time to process. Please hear me clearly. Sometimes it's okay to withdraw from your wife—if you're doing so in a mature and beneficial way. Some men have good motives for withdrawing. You or your wife will occasionally need time to process a situation alone before addressing it with each other. You know that your words will be harsh and angry in the heat of the moment, and you know your conversation will be better if you wait until you feel calmer. Especially if you're the one who doesn't want to do something, you may just need time to think, process your thoughts and the input from your spouse, and most importantly, to pray.

The need to process thoughts on your own, away from your wife, is greater for you than for your wife. Gary Thomas, in his book *Sacred Marriage,* describes a key biological difference that affects the way men and women process emotional matters. "Neurological studies show that men may take up to seven hours longer than women to process complex emotional data."[2] This explains why Scott has said things like "I really can't process any more" or "You machine-gun me when I walk in the door. I just can't handle that." The need to take time to process emotional information is valid, but it is not an excuse to avoid intimacy with your wife.

Here's the key: Communicate clearly to your wife that you need a time-out and that you want to talk later. If you do not communicate up front why you need some time to process some thoughts and feelings, your silence will feel hurtful or punishing. Agree on a time to come back together to talk about the issue, and then be a man of your word and make sure you really do talk.

God wants us to seek peace in our marriages, but not peace at all costs. If you avoid talking about difficult issues, you're avoiding healthy intimacy with your wife.

7. Say I'm sorry. Two of the most healing and restorative words in marriage are *I'm sorry.* Be the first to say these words and mean them. Don't let pride keep you from bringing harmony and healing to your marriage. If you're the offended spouse, be willing to say, "I forgive you."

Words of Death or Life

This chapter has been challenging to write. Scott and I are still learning how to practice many of these ideas in our own marriage. This year has been stressful as we've dealt with health issues, Scott's two jobs, raising our sons, speaking and writing, walking with close friends who have faced serious issues, and the daily ups and downs of life. I said to someone recently that this year has brought more stress than ever before, but Scott and I have also grown closer than ever. One reason is that we've had to communicate on some really big issues.

Learning to communicate in a way that draws you and your wife closer to each other will be a lifelong journey. You don't have to practice these communication tools all at once. Talk to God about what you've read, talk to your wife, and try some each day. Ask God what will draw you and your wife closer together.

As we end this chapter, I want to remind you of the key verse I mentioned when we began. "The tongue can bring death or life; those who love to talk will reap the consequences" (Proverbs 18:21 NLT). Scripture gives plenty of evidence that God's words have the power of life. In Genesis we're told God created every inch of the world with His spoken words. John 1:1 tells us that Jesus is the Word. Throughout the Gospels, Jesus heals countless people with the power of His words. Clearly, God's words have power, and God's desire is for our words to accomplish much also—particularly in our marriages. He wants our words to bring life to our marriages. We can choose what we will sow—words of life or words of death—and we will reap the consequences many times over.

I'll end with what I'll call "words of life" and "words of death." The words of life you speak today can move you one step closer to your wife, but words of death will move you away from her. May your words be a blessing to your wife and to your marriage.

Words of Life

I love you.

It's going to be okay.

Do you want to talk?

I always have time for you.

I appreciate how hard you work.

You are an incredible wife and mother.

You are more beautiful today than ever.

You have great insight.

I'm glad we talked about this.

Thank you for sharing with me what was on your heart.

I'm really looking forward to going out with you.

I'm sorry.

I was wrong.

Will you forgive me?

Thank you.

I understand.

I'm blessed to be your husband.

Words of Death

Why do you go on and on when you're talking about something?

Why do you have to talk so much?

You are such a nag.

Get off my case.

That's crazy (or stupid, clueless, dumb, or silly).

Don't ask me so many questions.

Why don't you just do what I told you to do?

I told you so.

That makes no sense.

Why is everything such a big deal to you?

You're just like your mother.

You are way too emotional.

Why did I ever marry you?

We'd be better off divorced.

PRAYER GUIDE

Heavenly Father,

I am thankful for You, Lord, my most steadfast Friend, and I am thankful for the friendship you've given me with my wife. Let my words to my wife and about my wife draw us closer to one another and never pull us apart. Teach me how to communicate with my wife in the way she needs. If any pride, stubbornness, selfishness, or any other sin is preventing good communication in our marriage, Lord, I confess that right now. Show me today what steps I can make toward my wife to listen to and talk with her the way she needs. Keep my heart willing to respond to her communication needs. Make me aware of any words of death I've spoken in our marriage, and as the Holy Spirit brings those to my mind, help me confess and turn from them, especially any words of divorce. Break any curse on our marriage from hurtful, angry, destructive words.

I want to speak words of life in my marriage, knowing that my words have power to accomplish great things. Guided by Your wisdom and love, may our communication build a protective wall around our marriage, a wall so strong that no temptations can weaken or crumble it. Amen.

5

You *Can* Understand Your Wife

One of our first plane trips to Scott's hometown in Minnesota illustrated that we had a long way to go toward understanding one another. As we landed in Minneapolis, we looked out the window, and Scott excitedly announced, "That's the Metrodome!" I knew by the way he stared at me expectantly that whatever he had just told me was a huge deal. And I remembered that he had told me that the largest mall in America was right there in Minneapolis, but I was pretty sure he hadn't called it the Metrodome. I had no idea what he was talking about, and I wasn't sure what I was supposed to say, so I went with the most honest response I could come up with: "What's that? And where's the mall?"

Now that we've been married 18 years and I have learned the importance of the Minnesota Vikings, I'm surprised Scott didn't send me back to the South then and there. He reached deep down inside himself and calmly and patiently explained to me the wonders of the Metrodome. Meanwhile, we completely bypassed the mall, unbelievably to me, to drive three hours north to his hometown in Backus, Minnesota. I have to commend Scott for his patient understanding of my lack of knowledge about the Metrodome. I'll also commend myself for not making a fuss about *being in the same city as the largest mall in America and not even going inside!*

From the day we commit to our spouses, we need to learn to understand them. The process begins when we're dating and will continue every day of our marriages. This whole book is about understanding your wife's needs, and this chapter will help you understand some unique aspects of a woman's makeup.

As I have mentioned, when I ask women what they need from their husbands, their number one answer has to do with communication. The second most frequent response is that a wife needs understanding. Despite what you sometimes may think, you really *can* understand your wife, and she *needs* you to understand her. In fact, 1 Peter 3:7 commands husbands to understand their wives: "You husbands in the same way, live with your wives in an understanding way, as with someone weaker, since she is a woman; and show her honor as a fellow heir of the grace of life, so that your prayers will not be hindered."

We should begin by agreeing on the definition of the word *understand. Understanding* in this chapter does not mean that your wife makes complete sense to you or that her actions are completely logical to you. It doesn't mean that you have her all figured out.

When I refer in this chapter to understanding your wife, I mean that you accept her with love, compassion, and sympathy. It's the sense behind this comment: "I understand you've had a hard day. Do you want to talk about it?" Understanding your wife means being empathetic by identifying with her situation, feelings, and thoughts.

God requires husbands to maintain an understanding attitude. Notice the consequence in the verse in 1 Peter: If you don't treat your wife with understanding, your prayers will be hindered. That's a serious consequence. All of your prayers will be hindered (not just prayers for your marriage) when you lack an understanding attitude toward your wife. That's pretty strong motivation for seeking to understand your wife.

Before we move on, I want to address a word in the 1 Peter passage that causes some controversy: the word *weaker*. That word sometimes has a connotation of being inferior, but as this passage makes clear, that's not what God meant. This passage is about honoring one another, so any sense of male superiority would be illogical here. God clearly designed men and women uniquely, but the differences have nothing to do with superiority or inferiority. The differences between men and women will inevitably create challenges as we try to understand one another, but the way we approach one another is of upmost importance to God. God made us different by design so we could complement one another in marriage.

One evening Scott and I watched a movie that included a scene in which a man and woman were arguing. They clearly didn't understand each other, and the man finally said, "Put the cuckoo back in the clock!" Scott and I laughed because we could both relate. Sometimes I do seem a little crazy to Scott, especially when the very words that pleased me yesterday make me irritable today. Or when I can't understand why he would want to make room in the budget to join a hunting club that he could meet with only a few times a year. When we need to lighten up a disagreement, one of us might say, "Put the cuckoo back in the clock."

We have all laughed at some time about the differences between men and women, but we can take this type of joking too far. If we believe that understanding one another is impossible, we won't be very motivated to be compassionate when our mates require empathy from us. We'll give up before we start, thinking we could never see eye to eye. Then our actions will reflect our attitudes. We'll be stuck in misunderstanding and isolation instead of creating bridges to oneness and unity. Thoughts, attitudes, actions—a powerful threesome. Proverbs

23:7 affirms the power of our thoughts: "As he thinks within himself, so he is." The thoughts we repeat to ourselves will direct our attitudes and actions. As you read this chapter, be aware of any thoughts that prevent you from understanding your wife, and ask God to fill you with a desire and ability to understand her.

Understand Your Wife's "Things Girls Don't Like" List

I've become more purposeful recently about teaching my two sons how to behave like gentlemen around girls. We have an ongoing dialogue, and I'm creating an ongoing "Things Girls Don't Like" list. Girls don't like...

1. burps and farts and stinky feet
2. dirty fingernails
3. unclipped toenails
4. BO
5. being told they look okay or fine (They want to be told they look pretty or beautiful or gorgeous or awesome.)
6. guys who talk on and on about sports, Xboxes, or guns
7. being shoved or patted hard (like a guy)

That's the list so far, and we'll continue working on it. I want my sons to learn that they cannot treat a girl like one of the guys. I explain that a girl is a girl, and she has some unique girl needs. I like to remind them how fortunate they are to have a mother writing this book about the needs of females. They'll have insights about women that will one day make them great husbands. (I haven't sensed their appreciation yet.)

The "Things Girls Don't Like" list is amazingly true for grown women too, but I've added a few things for husbands to remember. As God asks you to be sensitive to your wife's girl-ness, her femininity, remember that He designed the differences, and they come as no surprise to Him. Also, when talking about all females, I'm making some generalizations. Many of these preferences will apply to your wife, but some will not. And if I've missed something or am way off, at least this will help you pray about being sensitive to your wife's specific needs.

Many women are offended by bad smells, especially if those smells are coming from their husbands. In general women are more attuned to and affected by their environment, and that includes aromas. I'll be very honest: If Scott and I are sitting on the couch watching TV, and I smell some unpleasant odors coming from him, that is a turn-off to me and will likely turn me off from getting physically closer later.

Along the same lines, be aware of your personal hygiene. If you're sweaty, take a shower before sitting on the furniture or getting into bed, and brush your teeth. Take time to be clean. Really. I know this may seem like an unnecessary statement of the obvious, but it never hurts to remember that women are more sensitive to a lack of cleanliness.

Many women are repelled by harsh words. Vulgar, rough, slang language can really offend a woman. Off-color jokes and cursing are likely to be distasteful to her. Be careful how you talk, and follow the guidelines in Ephesians 5:4 (AMP): "Let there be no filthiness (obscenity, indecency) nor foolish and sinful (silly and corrupt) talk, nor coarse jesting, which are not fitting or becoming; but instead voice your thankfulness [to God]."

As I'm writing this section, I'm thinking about something I yell at my boys in a tone of voice that is both serious and teasing. If they do something they know they're really not supposed to do, such as burp aloud as one recently did in church, I might say, "Quit acting like you were born in a barn!" Or I could say, "You act like you don't have any home trainin'!" Both of these admonitions usually illicit at least a guilty smile, and I get my point across. Let me admonish you too. Act like a gentleman around your wife. Show some manners, courtesy, and sensitivity to her femininity. Know what offends her and avoid those behaviors.

Understand Your Wife's Need to Feel Beautiful

In the third grade my twin sister and I got to wear what was the height of grown-up-ness: go-go boots. Somehow we talked our granny into buying a pair for each of us. They were white with a bit of a heel, they zipped up the side, and they came just below the knee. They were super-cool! I remember the first night we wore them out to dinner. We didn't just walk in those boots—we pranced. After dinner we strutted around in those boots, laughing and dancing like little girls do. The grown-ups were laughing with us and saying how cute we looked. It was an intoxicating feeling to be looked at and admired.

But in the blink of an eye, everything changed. An older relative rebuked us sharply: "That's enough. Quit showing off like that and come sit down."

We were crushed, shamed, and deflated. How quickly we transitioned from feeling beautiful and proud to feeling ashamed and wanting to hide. Let me assure you, grown-up girls feel much the same way little girls do. Women want to know they're beautiful, but more quickly than you can imagine, they find themselves falling short of some unattainable standard. Wives need to feel beautiful, especially in their husband's eyes. They often look to their husbands to answer the question, am I beautiful?

I want to be careful not to be misunderstood because of the many distortions of beauty in our society. When I refer to beauty, I am not referring at all to the world's idea of perfection. Nor do I mean to imply that a woman's worth is based on her physical appearance. The beauty I'm referring to has to do with a woman's entire being. In other words, a woman's beauty is her essence, her outer beauty as well as her inner beauty. Both are crucial parts of who she is.

I remember a young couple I met early in my twenties. Even before they were married, the young man began to tear away at his fiancée's sense of beauty. One day I was part of a group of women who were asking the engaged girl about her wedding plans. As the conversation continued, the engaged girl explained that her fiancée had asked her to lose ten pounds before the wedding, so she had begun running and was trying to lose weight. Apparently this young man expected his future wife to attain to certain standards of outer beauty.

I was absolutely shocked, but I didn't know her and the other women in the group well enough to say anything. All I could think was, *The nerve of that guy!* I wondered how that made this young lady feel to find herself already measured and found lacking by the man she'd spend the rest of her life with. How crushed her heart must have been, even if she didn't acknowledge the hurt. How was he going to respond if she gained weight? What was he going to think as she grew larger during pregnancy? Would he still think she was beautiful as she aged?

Every woman understands the feelings behind the question that makes every man sweat: "Do these pants make me look fat?" The answer each and every time, dear husband, is this: "You look beautiful." Don't tell a woman she looks okay, and don't tell her she looks fine. You might as well just say she looks big as a house because that's what *fine* means to a woman. Tell her she looks beautiful or pretty. And if the pants really do make her look fat, let her best friend tell her. Here's the question she's really asking: *Husband, do you think I'm beautiful?* Let your answer always be yes.

God designed you to respond to your wife's beauty and even to want her to be beautiful. He intended for men to respond to visual beauty, and your desire to have an attractive wife is one of your deepest needs.

Be careful, however, of your physical standards for her. If you find your wife is no longer attractive to you for whatever reason—maybe you're just bored with your relationship, maybe you've let your expectations become distorted, or maybe she's let herself go—take these thoughts and feelings to God and ask Him to shape your expectations of your wife. If she needs to eat better and get some exercise, proceed carefully and cautiously when speaking to her about this. Pray about it, pray for her to have a desire to take care of herself, and pray for you to have physical passion for your wife alone. If you get a green light from God to talk to her about this matter, do so gently and tenderly. Remember that every one of us, men and women, are influenced by our culture's distorted definition of physical beauty. Be a godly husband, and don't let society shape your view of your wife's beauty. Let God.

Understand That Her Emotions Are Essential Parts of Her

Most of us will agree from our experience that women tend to be more openly emotional than men. God designed us uniquely male and female, and one of the unique aspects of a man, as we discussed in chapter 4, is that he can usually compartmentalize his thoughts and feelings more readily than a woman can or even wants to. To a woman, everything is connected, and her proclivity to connect plays a huge role in her emotions. Many factors affect her emotional state— a conversation from a day ago, a difficult project at work, a friend who's having troubles, her hormones, her bad hair day, challenges with the children, and even too much laundry to do.

She needs to express her emotions of happiness, sadness, hurt, anger, and fear to you, and she needs you to try to understand. Yes, I said try. Sometimes her feelings will make sense to you, and sometimes they won't. But remember how I defined understanding—a sense of empathy and identification. Your wife needs to know that you are reaching out to her in love, that you care, and that you want to connect with her.

How do you respond when you think your wife is being really emotional, maybe even overly emotional? Sometimes a man is extremely uncomfortable with his wife's display of emotions. He's not sure how to respond, so he may just withdraw from her. A wife will be hurt and offended if her husband does this. Or he might shame her for feeling what she feels. This response will hurt her to the core of her being. When a man tells his wife she's crazy for feeling what she feels, he belittles her. Alternatively, the husband might go into fix-it mode.

But a wife needs her husband's listening ear more than she needs his solution.

Adam and Eve were "naked and not ashamed." One of the implications of this is that a husband and a wife are to be emotionally open and vulnerable with each other. Your wife needs to know that she can safely express her emotions with you, as Jenni Wilson explains:

> I am weepy and emotional about people I love. My husband, Andy, provides a mental and physical shoulder for me to cry on. When I am feeling emotional, I need reassurance from Andy that everything will be okay. Andy is a safe place where I can voice my fears. I need the comfort of his reassurance. Issues with children, sickness, misunderstandings with friends…he is there to tell me things will be okay. The bottom line is that I know he understands where all true assurance lies. He relies on God, the one true Comforter, so his reassurance has authority and comforts me.

When your wife tells you how she feels, she's putting her heart in her hands and holding it out to you. If you don't respond in an understanding way, you take her heart from her hands, throw it on the ground, and stomp on it. She'll offer her heart to you less and less often, and eventually, her heart may harden toward you. If you don't purposefully try to express empathy, kindness, and understanding to your wife, you will create hurt and distance in your marriage instead of building oneness and closeness.

You are probably learning what kind of response will make your wife feel understood. When I am upset about something, I feel understood when at the end of a conversation Scott says, "It's all going to be okay." I actually learned this from observing my friends Catherine and Ron. When I heard Ron say that to Catherine, I thought, *That's it! That's what I need to hear to feel as if Scott understood me.*

Now, let me point out that this is an understanding response only after Scott has listened. If he just said this to me without listening first,

I would feel dismissed. I would feel as if my feelings were unimportant to him and I wasn't important enough to listen to.

Ask God to help you understand how to make your wife feel understood. A hug helps some women to feel understood. A certain phrase might be more reassuring to others. As we discussed in an earlier chapter, one of the most important ways you can demonstrate an understanding attitude toward your wife is by simply listening. Even if you don't completely understand, your efforts will communicate that you care, and that matters most to your wife. After all, sometimes we women don't know exactly what we need to hear. Marriage is a journey of discovering yourself and your spouse. As you surrender your heart to God and pray about understanding your wife, He will make you sensitive to her particular needs in this area.

In the previous chapter I offered lists of "words of life" and "words of death." Here are some sentences you can use to help your wife feel understood:

- Let's sit down and talk about this. I want to understand.
- You seem to have had a great day (or bad day). Tell me about it.
- I can tell this really hurt you. Do you want to talk? How can I pray for you?
- I don't have time right now, but I'll be home tonight, and I want to hear what you have to say.

On the other hand, here are some sentences that would make her feel misunderstood:

- I can't believe how emotional you are.
- Why can't we ever talk about things calmly?
- What on earth is wrong with you?
- If you didn't get so worked up about things, we could have a normal conversation.
- Women! Who can understand them!

Understand Her Personality Type

Have you ever just wanted your wife to change? Have you ever thought with frustration, *Why does she do that?* I spent many years telling Scott and God what they could do to change Scott and thus improve our marriage. Surrendering my marriage to God has included asking God how He wants me to change instead of telling Him how to change Scott.

Learning that we don't need to change one another has been a process for Scott and me. We experienced a turning point when we took a class about the different personality types. We learned that every person tends to fall in one of four personality types. Most people have a primary personality type and a secondary personality type. Understanding your wife's personality type will help you understand what makes her tick. Scott and I learned, as many couples will also, that our personality types are completely opposite. This understanding has helped us to accept our differences instead of trying to change one another. In *Personality Plus for Couples,* Florence Littauer explains the four personality types.

The sanguine types, also called the "popular personalities," are the "fun-loving, sunny, outgoing personalities who draw people to them because they seem to be having such a good time...Sanguines seek attention, affection, approval, and acceptance of those around them."[1] Sanguines are adventurous, active, talkative, and social. They are often the life of the party. Each personality type has positive and negative aspects. Sanguines tend to avoid anything that's not fun, such as housework, paperwork, and getting organized. They do not pay attention to details, they run late to appointments, and they often do not finish projects.

The second personality type, the melancholy or "perfect personality," is the direct opposite of the sanguine personality, and we often find these two married to one another. The melancholy is "deep, thoughtful, introspective, serious, and perfectionist."[2] Melancholies will get the job done and get it done right. They can be very sensitive, get their feelings hurt easily, be critical because of their perfectionist tendencies, and tend toward depression.

The third personality type is the choleric or "powerful personality." When you think of this type of person, think of take-charge leaders. "They strive for control and expect credit for their achievements. They love being challenged and easily accept difficult assignments. Their self-discipline and ability to focus make them strong leaders. But their drive and determination can cause them to become workaholics, make them opinionated and stubborn, and leave them insensitive to other's feelings."[3]

Lastly, there's the phlegmatic, the "peaceful personality." Cholerics and phlegmatics are often married to one another because the take-charge choleric is drawn to the compliant phlegmatic. Phlegmatics tend to be easygoing, laid-back, stable, and pleasant. As for the negative traits, they may procrastinate, avoid risk, and seek peace at all costs.

This summary of the four personality types gives you the groundwork for understanding your wife's personality type. Whether she's planning a dinner party, doing housework, or disciplining children, you will see her demonstrating some characteristics of these personality types. Regardless of the combination of personality types you find in your marriage, God knew that you and your wife could complement one another. Of course, if you resist the differences, you are likely to bring strife and disharmony into your marriage.

Each personality type includes strengths and weaknesses. For example, the take-charge choleric can learn to relax with the phlegmatic. The disorganized sanguine can learn from the melancholy's efficiency, and so on. Marriage partners must learn to give and take, and as they respond to one another in understanding, they grow closer.

Understand What Pushes Her Buttons

We happen to own an industrial-strength shredder. I'm quite sure it would shred our 75-pound dogs if they were unfortunate enough to catch their tails in that scary machine. When we first got the shredder,

I showed my sons the machine and told them that under no circumstances were they to use it and that they shouldn't even think about pushing its buttons. I could just see them losing some minor body part, like a hand, if they did.

Your wife has buttons you *must not push,* just as our shredder has buttons my sons should not push. If you do, you might lose a hand or maybe something even more vital, like your head. Even more importantly, you will lose the well-being your wife feels when you respect these particular buttons.

My particular button is visual clutter. Our kitchen is the first room we walk into when we enter our house from the garage. If debris is spread out on the counters, my stress level escalates the minute I see it. Unfortunately, men don't carry purses to contain their stuff, so Scott had a habit of emptying his pockets, flight bag, and computer onto the kitchen counters. I can't express how much this bothered me, especially if I had just cleaned up. I felt as if he had just undone all my efforts, and worse yet, he seemed not to appreciate my hard work around the house.

Scott's button is recycling. It's important to him—really, really important. And guess where he piles his recycling items—on the kitchen counters. You can imagine how that didn't work too well for us. Yes, recycling clutter bothers me on some days more than others, but in general, it bothers me a lot more to have that stuff collecting on the counters.

This recycling issue is a small one, but little things add up quickly in a marriage. All our quirks—good and bad, heartwarming and irritating—become the focus of our attention as we consider living with this other person's habit for the rest of our lives. What was once a small pinpoint of light now becomes an obnoxious floodlight. He leaves the toilet seat up, and she leaves tools on the workbench. One wife told me in a frustrated tone of voice that when her husband packed his lunch for work each day, he left bread crumbs on the counter. Every. Single. Morning.

We can each think of a little thing that drives us pretty crazy.

Marriage is so daily—day in and day out, we can choose to be considerate of another's whims, quirks, desires, and preferences. We can also choose not to be so considerate. Much of marriage is learning to compromise, learning to say to yourself, *If it makes her feel loved, I'll adapt.* Sometimes we need to ask ourselves if the issue really matters in the long run. And sometimes the small things really do matter, and that's when you work it out together in a way that suits you both.

Understanding Can Be Challenging

I had a conversation the other day with a good friend of ours. Mostly, I talked, and he listened as I gave him unsolicited marriage advice. In the course of our conversation, he said something we all think at times: *I know what you're saying is true, but sometimes it's so hard!* Yes, understanding one another's needs and being willing to respond to them can be difficult.

At times I want to hold a grudge against Scott rather than forgive, I want to have things my way rather than compromise, and I just want to be angry rather than try to understand. I always have to go back to God with my thoughts and feelings. When I do this, I'm reminded of who I really am and who I want to be—a woman who is shaped and molded by God and who reflects Him.

In the same way, the husband who wants to give up, who wants to say it's too hard, who wants his wife to be the one to change, who even thinks about walking out—that man is not the real you. The real you is the person God created you to be. A man who hungers and thirsts for God, a man who continues to seek God and to be transformed by the Holy Spirit from the inside out. I love the way The Message confirms this: "We see the original and intended shape of our lives there in him" (Romans 8:29 MSG). You discover the real you as you abide in Christ.

I discussed earlier in this chapter the importance of our thoughts and the way they influence our perspective of our spouses and our marriages. To have the marriage God wants you to have, you must become conscious of your thoughts. "We are destroying speculations and every lofty thing raised up against the knowledge of God, and we are taking every thought captive to the obedience of Christ" (2 Corinthians 10:5). Fill your mind with God's truth: You are the man He chose to love your wife for Him.

If you continually think to yourself, *I can't understand her...she needs to change...this marriage is too hard...*then you won't understand, you won't change, and your marriage will not be what God wants it to be. Take those frustrated or desperate thoughts captive to the Lord, confess them as sin, repent, and fill your mind with God's truth. Replace that "stinkin' thinkin'" with what God says. Have a dialogue with God in the heat of the moment: *Lord, You say that I can do all things through Your power that works in me* [Philippians 4:13]. *Lord, You tell me to be kind to my wife, tenderhearted, and forgiving* [Ephesians 4:32]. *Lord, I choose to replace my angry and hurt thoughts with Your thoughts. I want to obey You.*

As I remember the conversation I had recently with my friend, I also remember what he was like when he was first married. I see the changes he's made as he's grown in his faith. He's made a conscious effort to grow into the kind of man God wants him to be, and in doing so he's becoming the husband his wife needs. We're each a work in progress, changed by the Holy Spirit moment by moment and day by day as we keep our hearts surrendered to the One who loves us most.

PRAYER GUIDE

I'll include two prayer guides. The first is a prayer of St. Francis of Assisi, who lived in the twelfth century. His prayer reflects so well what it means to be God's heart and hands in this world.

Lord, make me an instrument of your peace.
Where there is hatred, let me sow love;
where there is injury, pardon;
where there is doubt, faith;
where there is despair, hope;
where there is darkness, light;
where there is sadness, joy.

O Divine Master, grant that I may not so much
    seek to be consoled as to console;
to be understood as to understand;
to be loved as to love.

For it is in giving that we receive;
it is in pardoning that we are pardoned;
and it is in dying that we are born to eternal life.

Lord,

I've learned in this chapter how important it is to my wife that I understand her. I ask that You give me the desire to understand her and accept her rather than change her. Lord, sometimes she's so different from me that I find myself frustrated. Forgive me when I act impatient or irritated toward her, and give me Your love so I will want to understand her. Give me wisdom and discernment to empathize with her and care for her in the way she needs. Help me to understand my wife. I ask that my wife and I truly become better together than we are as individuals. Let our commonalities and differences bring unity to our marriage rather than division. Let me treasure my wife the way You do, Lord. Amen.

6

Attitude Adjustment

Only one month after we opened Carolina Courts, I already needed an attitude adjustment. You've probably been there too—you know God doesn't want you to hold on to your negative attitude, but still you struggle to let go of it. This past Saturday I woke up feeling tired of many things: tired of seeing my husband only at the gym, tired of boys and dogs and dirt, tired of being supportive, and tired of being tired. You get the idea. I didn't want to have the thoughts I was having, so I wrestled in prayer with my attitude. *Lord, I know You don't want me to dwell on these thoughts about my marriage, and I know You don't want me to express them to Scott right now. I know he's doing the best he can do and that he's working hard to make this business a success. Lord, I pray You will change my attitude.*

I continued to pray throughout the day, including the drive to Carolina Courts with my sons. As I walked into a busy and crowded gym, I knew that my heart and my attitude still weren't where they needed to be. I went to find Scott to ask him where the boys and I were to work. When I found him, I took one look at the most tired face I'd ever seen on him, and my heart immediately softened. God answered my prayers about my attitude adjustment exactly when I needed Him to, and He gave me just the right portion of His love, mercy, and grace for Scott. I found out that this particular day had been a hard one for Scott. Along with being super busy, he'd been blasted by complaining customers. I tried to encourage him by reminding him of the feedback from most of our customers, which had been extremely positive.

What would I have done if I hadn't been praying about my attitude? I would have gone to the gym that day and made a point of telling Scott how tired I was with everything. I would have added more weight to his already heavy burden. I'm so thankful that's not what happened. It was a good reminder to me that as I trust the Lord and seek Him, He will provide.

Our attitude provides an accurate litmus test for the true condition of our hearts. As I've discussed throughout this book, God cares first about the condition of our hearts. One of many verses that remind us of this is Deuteronomy 5:29: "Oh that they had such a heart in them, that they would fear Me and keep all My commandments always, that it may be well with them and with their sons forever!" When God has our hearts, He knows that we're surrendered to Him. He'll mold us and shape our attitudes and actions to reflect His character. This verse also points out that the condition of our hearts not only affects our own lives but also has consequences for our families: "that it may be well with them and with their sons forever."

Our attitude can be like an odor spreading throughout our lives. One day I opened my car door and was blasted with a horrific smell. I searched every inch of the car but could not find the source of the stench. I then took action to get rid of the smell: I scrubbed the carpet with deodorizers and sprayed air freshener. The stench persisted, however.

I left the car doors open, deciding I couldn't possibly run errands in that stinky car. I went back inside, opened the refrigerator, and noticed a small trickle of milk had leaked onto the shelf. After examining the milk container, I saw that the milk must have leaked into the car the day before when I got groceries. That explained the cause of my stinky car: spoiled milk, one of the most offensive odors I've ever smelled. Negative attitudes are like the stench of spoiled milk, permeating our homes and affecting everyone.

Now imagine a pleasing aroma. What comes to mind? A freshly baked pie, the scent of the ocean, freshly brewed coffee, or a cinnamon candle. A pleasant aroma is so powerful that it can even bring a smile to our faces and make us feel more positive. The same is true of our positive attitudes. In our marriages we can be like a fragrant aroma by adopting attitudes that please Christ. In fact, Paul teaches that we are a "fragrance of Christ" (2 Corinthians 2:15).

In this chapter we're going to look at several attitudes that are vital to a thriving marriage. I've included attitudes to which a wife is especially sensitive. This is not an exhaustive list, so as you read, ask God to reveal any other attitudes that will help your marriage. Ask Him to give you an attitude like Christ's. As Paul writes in Philippians 2:3-5 (NLT), "Don't be selfish; don't try to impress others. Be humble, thinking of others as better than yourselves. Don't look out only for your own interests, but take an interest in others, too. You must have the same attitude that Christ Jesus had."

A Wife Needs a Husband Who Is Humble, Not Prideful

First Corinthians 13:4 (NIV) says, "Love is patient, love is kind. It does not envy, it does not boast, it is not proud."

Jim and Melinda have been married ten years, and most people who know them would probably say they have a solid marriage. Jim is a good man in many ways. He's a hard worker, and others look up to him. He's the first one at church to volunteer to serve by cooking the barbeque lunch or stacking the chairs after the service. He's friendly, a great storyteller, and knowledgeable on many subjects. One day at a party, Jim started telling a funny story. Melinda joined in the story because it also involved her, adding some details she thought were funny. But then Jim told her to stop interrupting; he was the one telling the story. Melinda felt humiliated.

When Melinda and I talked about her marriage, she said she feels as if marriage isn't all she hoped it would be, and she's not sure what to do about these feelings. Melinda often feels lonely and dismissed. When Jim comes home from work, he grabs the mail and barely responds as Melinda tries to chat with him. He expects Melinda to have dinner on the table soon after his arrival. While they eat dinner, he barely engages with her. In fact, many times he wants the TV on during dinner even though Melinda has repeatedly told him that really bothers her. After dinner, Melinda cleans up the kitchen while Jim heads down to the basement, and she might not see him for the rest of the night. When Melinda cautiously mentions that she'd love his company, he becomes defensive: "I'm tired of you always saying that. After a long day I need a break."

I asked her if she ever talks to Jim about the way she feels, and she quickly responded, "Not anymore. I've tried in the past, but it doesn't do any good. He just gets mad at me and tells me he's tired of me always having issues. It's Jim's way or the highway. I've learned it's easier to just let it go. He can be the friendliest, nicest, and most giving person to anyone but me. If people knew what he was like at home, they'd be surprised. I'm beginning to resent that."

Jim is filled with pride. That might not seem obvious to people outside their home, but to Melinda it's painfully obvious. I'm starting this chapter by focusing on an attitude that is undoubtedly the most challenging: humility. It's a good starting point because the opposite of humility, pride, can be one of the most destructive attitudes in marriage. Pride divides; humility binds. Pride creates distance; humility fosters oneness. Pride denies faults; humility admits weaknesses. Pride is self-reliant; humility depends on God and others. Pride is self-serving; humility serves others.

Do you have a prideful attitude toward your wife? See if any of these describe you:

- You tell your wife what to do rather than seeking her input, because God says you're the spiritual leader of the home.

- You don't help your wife with the kids and home because you're doing your job of providing a paycheck. The house and kids are her responsibility.

- You're tired of her nagging about her needs. They infringe on your time to work or do what you like to do.

- You think, *Why doesn't she see how unreasonable she's being?*

- You spend time pursuing your own interests or hobbies. After all, you work hard and deserve a break.

- You tell her ways to change and get frustrated when she doesn't.

- You wish she'd quit telling you her needs because not meeting them makes you feel like a failure.

As you ask God to make you humble, He will reveal the many disguises of pride: boasting, selfishness, rudeness, irritability, blaming others, having a critical spirit, self-absorption, arrogance, thinking you're always right, and superiority. All the varieties of pride are the very opposite of love. Without a humble attitude in your marriage, you might find your wife distant, unresponsive, or even giving up all hope for your marriage.

Pride will make you blind to your own sin, so take some time to examine yourself prayerfully. The best solution to be free of pride is to humble yourself before God (James 4:10). Your relationship with the Lord depends on your humble recognition that you are a sinner in need of His forgiveness, mercy, and love. As you grow in your relationship with Christ, He'll shape you and mold you to look more like Him, and you will develop the humble attitude of Christ.

Our society often mistakenly associates humility with weakness. Even Christian men can have a hard time understanding that humility really shows great strength of character, and more importantly, it's an attitude that reflects Christ. In fact, you can't be humble in your own strength. Humility requires a good dose of God's strength in you.

Here are some ideas for showing a humble attitude:

- Humble yourself before the Lord daily by confessing your sins and receiving God's forgiveness and love. Be the first one to say, "I'm sorry."
- Do something the way your wife wants it done.
- Volunteer for the humbling household duties—clean the toilets, change the diapers, wipe up the spit-up, pick up the dog poop.
- Make sure your tone of voice is free of sarcasm.
- Give up a day of doing what you want to do and devote yourself to doing what your wife wants to do.

A Wife Needs a Husband Who Is Positive, Not Negative

"A miserable heart means a miserable life; a cheerful heart fills the day with song" (Proverbs 15:15 MSG).

Do you know people you would rather not be around because they constantly complain and find fault? Negativity puts a damper on good times and makes hard times harder. Maybe you've become complaining, critical, complacent, grumpy, disagreeable, or unappreciative. Maybe you're not outright negative, but you don't go out of your way to be positive. You may need to become more purposeful about adopting a positive attitude, about being content, joyful, peaceful, happy, and agreeable. Your positive attitude will energize your marriage rather than drain it.

In an earlier chapter I discussed four personality types: sanguine, choleric, melancholy, and phlegmatic. We saw that choleric and melancholy personalities tend to be more negative than positive. This is not an excuse for you to be the way you are, especially if that means you're going to keep your grumpy attitude. It means you will have to consciously adopt new behavior patterns and partner with God to allow His Spirit to transform your character.

Thank your wife. Sometimes I've thought to myself, *Does Scott think the magic fairy cleans this house and does his laundry? He has no idea what my day is like and all I have to handle.*

Your wife does a lot of work that no one notices or appreciates. She does these things because she loves her family, but your words of thanks will put some pep in her step. Notice all the little things she does and thank her. Say the words, "I appreciate you. Thank you for fixing this delicious meal. Thank you for working so hard." Your wife especially needs your words of appreciation if you have small children. This is a very hands-on season of parenting, and those little ones usually don't express appreciation. Missy told me, "I need my husband to know that being a stay-at-home mom is the best job in the world, but it's also the hardest." Even when a wife is completely content with her life, she still needs appreciation from her husband.

Praise your wife. Another way to express a positive attitude is to praise your wife. I still remember the first professor to praise my writing—and that was a long time ago! I remembered those words many years later as I began to pursue writing more seriously. For some reason (and this drives my husband crazy), women need about ten compliments to make up for one critical comment. With criticism, your wife can easily become discouraged or insecure. Your compliments encourage her and bring out the best in her. She will feel motivated to press on instead of feeling defeated and worn out.

Be agreeable. Have you gotten into the bad habit of disagreeing? Then next time your wife makes a suggestion or has an idea, agree with her. Respond with, "Great! That sounds like a good idea. I'd love to."

Here are some ideas for showing a positive attitude:

- Begin your quiet time by thanking God for ten specific things.
- Thank God every day for your wife.
- Praise your wife for something specific about her character or something she does for you or the family.
- Have each one of your children write Mom a letter of appreciation.
- Say every day, "I love you, and I'm so glad I married you."
- Tell your children they have the best mom ever. Let your wife overhear you say this.
- Smile, laugh, and have fun.
- Don't complain. Don't whine. Don't be grumpy. Keep some negative things to yourself.
- Be your wife's cheerleader, not her critic.

A Wife Needs a Husband Who Is Kind, Not Inconsiderate

"Do not let kindness and truth leave you; bind them around your neck, write them on the tablet of your heart" (Proverbs 3:3).

In Galatians 5:22, we find a list of attributes called the fruit of the Spirit, a list that includes kindness. The number one place we need to show kindness is at home. It's easy to use up our kindness with others, and by the time we come home, our supply of kindness can be depleted. But we have a continual source of kindness in Christ. We bear the fruit of kindness as we abide in Christ. "I am the vine, you are the branches; he who abides in Me and I in him, he bears much fruit, for apart from Me you can do nothing" (John 15:5). One of the ways you can abide in Christ is by praying that Christ's kindness will flow through you at home.

Try this as you ask Christ to help you with your attitude. Picture Him seated on His throne. Go to Him; kneel before Him. Reach out your hands toward Him and place in His hands your worries, unfinished business, and concerns from the day at work. Leave with Him any attitudes—irritation, harshness, selfishness—that are detrimental to your relationship with your wife. Imagine Christ handing you a box. Open it up and take out the portion of His kindness (or other attitude) you need for your wife and children.

Consider these synonyms for the word *kind: considerate, thoughtful, tenderhearted, loving, sympathetic,* and *understanding.* Imagine what your marriage would be like if you made a priority of being kind to your wife. What would your marriage look like if you decided that the person you were going to be kindest to was your wife? I bet your marriage would make God smile! Let's look at some practical ways to show kindness in marriage.

Be considerate. Consider what matters to your wife, and make that as important to you as it is to her. Let me say that again—what matters to your wife should matter just as much to you. If cleanliness and order are important to her, pick up your clothes and put them in the hamper. Wipe the sink after shaving. If your wife wants your undivided attention, don't answer the phone or check e-mails while talking to her. Being considerate about small, daily concerns can make a huge difference in your marriage.

Go out of your way. One Mother's Day, Scott performed a grand act of kindness that still makes me smile as I think about it. He invited several of our couple friends over for dinner, and then he and the other guys cooked, served, and cleaned up the entire meal. Scott went all out, looking up new menus on the Internet, getting the groceries, grilling the fish, and creating a colorful, healthy, delicious meal for me and my girlfriends. That was a special treat and an all-out act of kindness.

Along with all the daily ways to show kindness, once in a while a husband needs to do something big. Ask God to show you a way to go all out in loving your wife by being kind. Clean the house. Plan a date, including getting the babysitter. Take her away for a night. Give her time to pursue her interests and friendships. Go out of your way to be kind in a sacrificial way.

Be gentle. Are your attitude and actions toward your wife like the blows of a sledgehammer or like a gentle breeze? One characteristic of kindness is gentleness—an attitude that women really respond to. Let God be your model in this. Sometimes I think men hesitate to show gentleness, fearing that they may appear weak. Notice, however, that God is both strong like a lion (Revelation 5:5) and tender like a lamb (John 1:29). When you show your wife gentleness by hugging her, caressing her, holding your children, praying aloud humble prayers, and speaking with a kind tone of voice, you bring out the gentleness in your wife too.

Here are some ideas for showing your wife kindness:

- Do a household chore that your wife would normally do, and don't point it out to her.

- Say please and thank you. Make manners a priority in your family.

- Fill your mind with God's truth: "Love is patient, love is kind" (1 Corinthians 13:4).

- If you can't say something nice, don't say anything at all.

- Commit to God and to your wife that you will never speak critically about her to others.

- Speak gently.

- Put your dirty clothes in the hamper and your dirty dishes in the dishwasher.

- Plan a surprise that will delight your wife.

- Talk with your family about ways to be kind and considerate.

A Wife Needs a Husband Who Is Gracious, Not Judgmental

"Above all, keep fervent in your love for one another, because love covers a multitude of sins" (1 Peter 4:8).

Cartilage is a tissue that is found in many places in our bodies, including at the end of bones where joints form. It protects our joints from wear and tear, helps them move smoothly, and absorbs shock. When the cartilage in our knee, for example, is damaged, we feel pain. Grace in our marriages is like the protective covering of cartilage in our joints. A husband who shows his wife a gracious attitude covers her with his understanding, protects the marriage from misunderstandings and short-tempered emotions, and helps his wife absorb life's jolts and shocks.

For example, the other day Scott came home late to discover that I had forgotten to turn off the hose after washing the dogs. The backyard was overflowing with water—an inconvenience and a costly mistake on my part. He could have gotten mad at me, but he didn't. His gracious attitude covered my shortcoming.

The verse at the beginning of this section contains the word *love* rather than the word *grace.* That's because one aspect of love is grace. It's the part of love that is generous, forgiving, encouraging, and unconditional. It's the part of love that empowers you to fill in the gaps rather than notice what's lacking in your wife. Grace asks, "How can I help you?" instead of growing frustrated or bitter when your wife isn't measuring up to your standard.

Bringing criticism, judgment, and self-righteousness into your marriage is all too easy. Saying "Why didn't you..." "You should have..." or "I told you so" requires no effort. But being gracious is what we need in marriage, and that's what Christ calls us to be. We're human. We're going to disappoint one another. We're not always going to meet each other's needs. When you are fully aware of your own weaknesses and of the ways you fall short of the glory of God, you are more likely to show your wife a gracious attitude. God's Word reminds us that "love covers." How can you cover your wife with the love of grace today?

Here are some ideas for showing a gracious attitude:

- Don't say, "I told you so."
- Let it go.
- Don't remind her of mistakes from her past.
- Assume the best.
- Don't say things like "Get off my case" or "You're such a nag."
- In your quiet time, think about the different ways God has covered you with grace rather than burdened you with judgment.
- Call your wife today just to tell her you love her and are praying for her.
- Hang around someone with a gracious attitude. Let his attitude rub off on you.

A Wife Needs a Husband Who Is Respectful, Not Dishonoring

"Be devoted to one another in brotherly love. Honor one another above yourselves" (Romans 12:10 NIV).

Do you have something you treasure? Maybe it's a sports trophy, a jersey from your glory days, a gun, fishing rod, a signed football or baseball, a truck or a car. Maybe it's something your grandfather or father passed down to you. If you prize something, you probably give it special treatment. You're careful with the way you handle it and make sure others are too. You spend extra time tending to it because you treasure it.

Now consider how you treat your wife. Does she get special treatment? One way to respect your wife is to treasure her. Scripture says that's exactly what she is—a treasure. "The man who finds a wife finds a treasure, and he receives favor from the LORD" (Proverbs 18:22 NLT). How can you make your wife feel treasured?

The males in my house humor me by treasuring me in a silly way. Zachary might say to me, "Mom, can I download a song?"

I'll answer, "Did you mean, 'Pretty, pretty princess, may I download a song?'"

Zachary will sigh (he's 14, thus the sigh) and call me "pretty, pretty princess," and I'll say yes to his request. Yes, every now and then I like to be called a "pretty, pretty princess." When my sons call me this—and every now and then my husband—I smile and feel treasured. Maybe your wife would like a special title name too. I'm sure you can think of other ways to cherish her. Maybe, like me, she'll even suggest one. Find a way to make her feel cherished, honored, and respected.

Another way to honor or respect your wife is to value her opinion. A wife is her husband's helper, so let your wife help you! You can do this by asking her input or advice in a situation. God may even ask you to follow it when it doesn't make complete sense to you or when you really don't want to. Recognize your wife's unique talents, gifts, and insights—they can be helpful to you and your marriage. Don't get into the bad habit of acting as if what she says is not worthy of your consideration. Your wife will feel dishonored and disrespected if you repeatedly dismiss her suggestions or advice.

Sometimes men are resistant to their wives' help because women can easily become controlling or manipulative, a curse from the sins of Adam and Eve (Genesis 3:16). Men hate to be nagged or told what to do, but maybe women nag because their husbands don't listen to their wives' good advice. Try listening more carefully, and maybe she will quit nagging! Your wife is not the Holy Spirit, but she can be your helper. Don't be so proud you think you don't need help.

Finally, you respect your wife when you value what's important to her. If she's told the kids they can't watch a certain TV show or go to a certain party, don't reverse her decision. If making sure the whole family eats healthily is a priority to her, then make that a priority yourself.

Kelly and Phillip recently told me about a situation when Phillip honored what was important to his wife. But it didn't happen all at once, as Phillip explains:

> Kelly is really into parenting right now. She thinks this is an area we can work on together by reading a book on parenting. Well, I know it's an area I can improve in, but I told her I just didn't want to read this book. I've just got a lot to do right now.

Kelly explained her thoughts:

> I was upset at Phillip's reluctance to read this parenting book because it's important to me, and I thought it should be important to him as well. If he loves me, and if we are "one flesh," then when he sees how passionate I am about this topic, my hope is that he would respect it.

Phillip continued:

> One of my first thoughts was, *I spend a lot of time with the kids—more than a lot of dads do.* I left town for work, and as I was driving, I kept thinking about this issue and how Kelly was upset. I prayed, *Lord, Kelly's expectations are so high! I don't want to read another book. I've got other books I'd rather read.* I sensed God was asking me what my priorities were. I also realized I was comfortable where I was and didn't want to make the effort to change. Then—and here's the clincher—I'm certain God said to me, *Calm down and listen to Kelly. Ninety percent of the time she's right.*
>
> Meanwhile, Kelly was at home, praying that the Lord would soften my heart on this parenting issue. I came back after being out of town, and we started discussing the issue

again. Truthfully, I fell asleep, which of course was the wrong thing to do! But the next day we discussed it some more, and I told Kelly I was willing to try the book and that I'd read it with a good attitude.

Notice that this issue took time, it took communication, and it required both Kelly and Phillip to pray that God would help them to honor one another.

Here are some ideas for showing a respectful attitude:

- Don't interrupt your wife when she's speaking.
- Ask your wife's opinion and follow her advice.
- Consult your wife before committing yourself to plans.
- Before correcting your wife about something, ask yourself if it really matters.
- Use a gentle and calm tone of voice. Avoid being harsh or demanding.
- Don't lecture her as if she's a child.
- If something is important to your wife, make it important to you.

A Wife Needs a Husband Who Is Forgiving, Not Hard-Hearted

> Since God chose you to be the holy people he loves, you must clothe yourselves with tenderhearted mercy, kindness, humility, gentleness, and patience. Make allowance for each other's faults, and forgive anyone who offends you. Remember, the Lord forgave you, so you must forgive others. Above all, clothe yourselves with love, which binds us all together in perfect harmony (Colossians 3:12-13 NLT).

How are you going to clothe yourself when you talk with your wife? Look back at this verse and note what clothes God commands you to put on. Song of Solomon 2:15 (NIV) refers to small offenses as little foxes: "Catch for us the foxes, the little foxes that ruin the vineyards." Don't let the little foxes ruin your marriage vineyard. What small offenses does your wife commit? Can you forgive her?

When I think of forgiveness, I think of Dan, who has forgiven his wife, Holly, for doing the same thing over and over. Holly has a hard time parking in their garage. It sits at a tricky angle, and she has run into the garage wall quite a few times. In fact, her van has plenty of scrapes and dents. Dan could have chosen many ways to respond— he could be angry every time, or he could berate her, but that's not his reaction. He has repeatedly chosen to forgive Holly.

Without forgiveness, you will become irritated, hard-hearted, bitter, and disconnected from your wife. A friend of mine taught me a way to make sure this doesn't happen: The *moment* I feel offended, I can choose to forgive. If your wife says something to you that makes you mad or hurt, begin praying at that very moment to forgive her. Doing this allows God to begin softening your heart immediately.

In addition to dealing with the little foxes of small offenses, we will sometimes need to forgive our spouses for big offenses. We might be betrayed by unfaithfulness, our trust might be rattled by secrets our spouses keep, or our feelings might be stomped on by spouses who do the same hurtful things over and over again. If one quality makes a Christian marriage stand out from the rest, it's our choice to forgive our spouses.

You will have countless occasions to forgive your wife simply because Christ commands you to. You might feel as if you're ignoring the offense or giving your stamp of approval by choosing to forgive. Your pride and fear might rise up: *What if the offense happens again and again? Will I be taken for a fool? What will others think?*

Choosing to forgive is an act of obedience to God's command. Forgiveness entails choosing over and over again not to dwell on the offense because that would allow a root of bitterness to grow in your heart. But let's be clear: If you're dealing with a big issue in your marriage, you can choose to forgive but still need to spend a great deal of time talking about the situation, praying separately and together, and seeking godly counsel to help you through the hard situation.

Let me share with you a response from a woman who forgave her husband's infidelity. I asked this woman, "How do you *not* get angry all over again when you remember the hurt your husband caused you?"

She replied, "I choose to believe that God loves me, my husband, and my children. And I choose to trust God." Her answer was simple but not easy. Forgiveness is a choice, not a feeling. It's one of the most essential attitudes for bringing life to your marriage, and it flows from your relationship with Christ.

Here are some ideas for showing a forgiving attitude:

- Dwell on Christ's forgiveness of your sins.
- Say to your wife, "I forgive you."
- Say, "I'm sorry."
- Choose not to dwell on your wife's hurtful words or actions.
- Don't hold a grudge or seek revenge.
- Choose your friends wisely. Be careful not to be around others who bad-mouth their spouses.
- Be a part of a small group or men's Bible study.

What if a stranger observed you only in your marriage relationship? What would this stranger discover about you? Imagine this person knows nothing about your job, children, hobbies, community involvement, or service at church. This person knows only what is revealed by your attitudes and actions toward your wife. This person's observations would be quite revealing, wouldn't they?

Perhaps this shows us one of the main purposes of marriage: to reveal our character. No one knows us like our spouses—we can never hide our true character from them. This unique intimacy is one of the reasons attitudes like grace and forgiveness are so necessary in marriage.

Once our character is brought to the light, little by little God uses the crucible of marriage to refine our character and to make us look more like Him. This is what spiritual maturity is all about. In Malachi 3:2 we're told that God is like a refiner's fire. Here is the way *The Life Application Study Bible* explains the purpose of this refining process:

> In the process of refining materials, the raw metal is heated with fire until it melts. The impurities separate from it and rise to the surface. They are skimmed off, leaving the pure metal. Without this heating and melting, there could be no purifying. As the impurities are skimmed off the top, the reflection of the worker appears in the smooth, pure surface. As we are purified by God, his reflection in our lives will become more and more clear to those around us.

God's refining process will help you leave behind any attitudes that hinder your marriage, and it will give you strength to embrace attitudes that help your marriage. It won't always be easy, but as you partner with God, He will bless your heart's desire and your efforts with His power. This is a fight worthy of your best efforts. Treasure your wife and treasure your marriage enough to "fight the good fight." In this process of being refined, hold tightly to God's love, a love that always wants what is best for you, for your wife, and for your marriage.

PRAYER GUIDE

Heavenly Father,

Create in me a clean heart, O God, and renew a steadfast Spirit within me [Psalm 51:10]. Search me, O God, and know my heart [Psalm 139:23]. Soften my heart and make me willing to receive an attitude adjustment from You, Lord. Help me to adopt attitudes that bring me closer to my wife. May they be like a fragrant aroma, pleasing to You. May they be what my wife needs. Help me to show her humility, a positive spirit, kindness, graciousness, respect, and a forgiving spirit. As the Holy Spirit reveals sinful attitudes in me, Lord, I confess them to You and ask that You work through me to show Your heart of love to my wife. I pray in Jesus' name. Amen.

7

Share the Journey

⁓∽⁓

During the first few years of our marriage, Scott taught math and coached several sports at Chamblee High School in Atlanta. Then he started flight school part-time right down the road at the DeKalb Peachtree airport. After that, he was a flight instructor while continuing to teach at the high school.

We both became accustomed to having busy lives, but when we had our first son, Zachary, things became much different for me. I wanted to be home more with the three of us sharing life and making memories. I continued to teach while Zachary was in daycare. I wasn't too happy about the daycare situation, but our modest teaching salaries and the high cost of flight school required our two incomes. We were both hoping I could someday be a stay-at-home mom.

Scott was hired by a small commercial airline, US Airways Express, and was based in West Palm Beach, Florida. By a fortunate turn of events, moving from Atlanta to Florida meant that we'd be living 15 minutes from my parents.

Scott and I both remember those three years in Florida as some of our happiest married years. We still weren't making much money and lived in a small townhouse, but the rewards of those years far outweigh any sacrifices. Scott felt fulfilled as his piloting career advanced, and I was happy being a mother and teaching at a private Christian school. Many afternoons Scott, Zachary, and I would head to the beach for a late afternoon of building sand castles and enjoying a picnic. My mom and dad were hands-on grandparents, and their home became like a second home for us.

After three years of what we fondly refer to as "the good old days," Scott's next career advancement was a dream come true—he was hired by a major airline, US Airways. This meant saying goodbye to my parents and some close friends and moving to Charlotte, North Carolina, a city where we knew no one. At this time our second son, Tyler, was only four months old, and this made the goodbyes especially heart-tugging. But we knew this day had been coming and hoped that Charlotte would become our home base for many years. We were thankful for the years we were able to live near my parents, but we were also thrilled with Scott's new job.

We loved Charlotte and found a church home the first week we were there. We lived in an apartment until we could figure out where we wanted to settle more permanently. For the first time I got to be a stay-at-home mom, and as Scott's dreams were coming true, so were mine.

Life was good, but for some reason, I wasn't as happy as I thought I'd be. In fact, I was lonely. Scott's new flying job took him away from home more than he'd ever been. He was typically gone four or five days in a row. Meanwhile, I was at home with two little ones in a town where I knew no one.

One day I was sitting at the little table in our Charlotte apartment with Zachary and Tyler. Scott called from out of town just to check in. I made the mistake of asking him what he was doing. He responded by telling me about the mouth-watering steak, loaded baked potato, and hot buttered bread he was enjoying on his expense account at a nice restaurant. I was eating the leftover chicken nuggets from Tyler's high-chair, and I can assure you that I was not sharing Scott's happiness over his meal.

During these days I felt resentment creeping into my heart. I was thankful for many things, such as both our dreams coming true and Scott being a great provider, but I was disappointed about some things too. I hated that Scott was gone so much. I missed my friends and parents, who had been such wonderful supports in Florida. In Charlotte I literally had no one to call for help and no friends to share the day with.

Our new situation in Charlotte presented some big challenges, and Scott and I didn't immediately know how to handle our new circumstances in a way that worked for both of us. I felt as if we were living separate lives. He did his flying thing, and meanwhile I held down the fort at home. By the time Scott got home, I was so worn-out that I wanted a break from life. We also wanted to have family time, but this left little time for us as a couple. I felt more and more disconnected from Scott, and consequently, more discouraged. Scott felt much the same, and he often said he missed me.

I didn't like feeling hurt, frustrated, or angry because of our disconnection, but only after lots of time and prayer was I finally able to put my thumb on the heart of the matter. The root of our problems was that I felt like a lone ranger most of the time, and I wanted to be a part of a team. I wanted to share more of life's journey with Scott.

As I've talked to women, they've expressed this need to share the journey of life with their husbands in a number of ways:

- "I need my husband to walk along beside me through the journey of faith, marriage, child rearing, and so on. I need him to really be a partner."
- "I need my husband to have a sense of awe, or at least a true appreciation, for the demands of my day."

- "I wish my husband realized that I love being a wife and mother, but I also have interests beyond that, and I want him to take an interest in those things."
- "I need my husband to be my friend—not the way a girlfriend is, just the way only my husband can be my friend."

I bet your wife would say a loud amen to at least one of these comments. Perhaps you and your wife can relate to what Scott and I experienced, feeling like lone rangers rather than feeling part of the same team. In marriage, both husband and wife must be committed to operating as a team. The more you follow this commitment with actions, the more you'll be united rather than isolated or disconnected.

Daily life provides many obstacles to a couple's teamwork. Maybe you both have full-time jobs outside the home, or maybe your wife works part-time. If your wife stays home and is a full-time homemaker and mother, she has a job that never ends. You love your children and want to make them a priority, but someone has to work and pay the bills. Meanwhile, you have daily chores to attend to. Beyond life's daily challenges, bigger issues will also threaten to tear apart your partnership: financial struggles, health issues, problems with children, and in-law problems, just to name a few.

A wife who feels as if she is alone or carrying too many responsibilities without her husband's supporting partnership will be discouraged, disheartened, or exhausted. On the other hand, a wife who feels that she and her husband are sharing life will have an open heart to her husband and her marriage. In this chapter we'll talk about some ways you and your wife can make sure you're a winning team.

Sharing the Journey by Being a Provider

Scott's work ethic is one of his most attractive qualities. Whatever job he has held—teacher, pilot, and now gym owner—he throws himself completely into that job. I feel enormously secure knowing Scott will work hard and that he will always provide for his family financially. In the same way, your wife needs to know that you will always be willing to work diligently to provide for your family.

As we talk about the husband's role of being a provider, let's be clear what God says. Genesis 2:15 says, "Then the LORD God took the man and put him into the garden of Eden to cultivate it and keep it." Adam stands as an example to all men that their role is to be providers for their families. The New Testament echoes this commandment in 1 Timothy 5:8: "But if anyone does not provide for his own, and especially for those of his household, he has denied the faith and is worse than an unbeliever." Adam and Eve were told to enjoy the garden, but after their disobedience, they were banished from the garden—one of the many consequences of their sin. Along with this consequence, Adam's work would require toil and sweat (Genesis 2:17-19). In other words, work would now be difficult for men.

One of the important ways a husband fulfills his role is by being a financial provider. Being a financial provider means providing income, and it also means managing the money by being a good steward. You and your wife can decide together who will actually make sure the bills get paid. A combined effort of setting a budget and living within it will work best and keep you working as a team rather than isolating you. Talk with your wife about tithing, purchases, savings, giving, and investments, and honor one another's desires.

I know of marriages in which the wife is the actual bill payer, though in our marriage, Scott is the one who manages the bills. This is a task that should naturally fall to the spouse who has the time and skills to manage your money in a way that honors God. Because there is so much misunderstanding about husband's and wife's roles, I want to add that while a man is to be a provider, this does not exclude his wife from also working. You and your wife must seek God to know what He wants you to do in this area.

God's Perspective of Work

Most men I've observed are willing to be the providers, but finding God's perspective about this role can be a challenge today. If you're like many of the men I know, you're a hard worker who wants what is best for your wife and children. I can't begin to imagine the burden of responsibility you carry daily, so I don't want to undermine your commitment to this role. I imagine that as a provider you feel as if you're often between a rock and hard place, wanting to provide financially but feeling the tug of many other responsibilities and of your wife's and children's needs.

Nevertheless, God's perspective honors balance. Many men work too much. They're workaholics, leaving their wives feeling like single parents, often lonely, hurt, and frustrated by their husbands' absence. Scripture encourages hard work but also warns us not to idolize money or its rewards. First Timothy 6:10 warns that "the love of money is a root of all sorts of evil, and some by longing for it have wandered away from the faith and pierced themselves with many griefs." What a wise verse to apply to your role as a provider.

Ask God to give you His perspective and to help you make financial decisions that honor your entire family, not your selfish desires or materialism. This may include examining how many hours you spend at work. Have you prayed about how much time God wants you to spend in the workplace and how much time you are at home?

Several men told me they feel enormous pressure because their wives spend more than they earn. If you're in this situation and you're living in debt, talk to your wife. Explain to her the pressure you feel, and work as a team to come up with a plan to live within your means. Debt can be a heavy burden in a marriage.

In chapter 1, I included a story from Mandy and Butch Ferguson's marriage. I want to continue their story here. Butch was a good provider for his family, but he was using material things as a Band-Aid for the other problems in their marriage. At one time Butch had a distorted view of being the provider.

> When problems arose in our marriage, I reminded myself that a bonus or a big commission check was right around the corner. I thought that money would take care of the problems we were having. In the meantime, I'd resort to "retail therapy" to make us happy. I wanted my family to have all the things other families like ours had—and more. Being able to purchase what we wanted felt great, but the feeling soon wore off, and I'd go right back to burying my head in the sand because the money issues popped back up.

Financial issues can add lots of stress to a marriage, threaten to tear you apart, and tempt you to attack one another because of your hurt and frustration. At the same time, addressing the financial issues alone is not necessarily the ultimate solution. For Butch and Mandy and many other couples, money issues can be symptoms of some deeper problems. Butch describes the way his eyes were opened to this during their first counseling session:

> At our first counseling appointment, Dan sat us down and began asking us questions about our relationship: Why are you here? How long have you been married? After only a few minutes, Dan asked me what I depended on Mandy for in our marriage. I told him that she is a great mother, keeps the house together, expresses love, and all the other things I should say. He then asked Mandy what she depended on me for in our marriage. Love, caring, affection, fathering, and intimacy were just a few of the responses that came to my mind. But at that very moment, without hesitation, Mandy hit me with a huge verbal left hook that landed square on the jaw and made my knees buckle. Without hesitation, Mandy simply said, "A paycheck."

That's it? I was merely a source of income to help her get through life? I was so stunned, a gorilla could have walked through the room and I wouldn't have seen it. The two words she uttered resonate with me still. How could I have missed the mark as a husband? In my eyes, my manhood just got reduced to a few measly bucks.

Butch provided financially, but this alone was not the answer. What did Mandy really need? If you review their story in chapter 1, you'll see Mandy was really looking for a partnership from Butch, not just a paycheck. She needed Butch to stop looking for a quick fix for their marriage issues.

Butch began to understand that though providing financially was a vital part of God's call for him to be the head of his family, he needed God's wisdom in this area, not his own. As Butch surrendered his marriage to God and allowed God to show him what it meant to be a provider, the marriage was transformed. Butch became the partner Mandy needed and the leader God wanted him to be.

Over the next few weeks, I began to see a change in Mandy and she in me. God was revealing to me that Mandy needed me to lead because she was tired of doing everything on her own. Our relationship had gotten to the point that if she wanted something done, she would just do it herself because it was easier that way.

As Mandy saw me begin to lead our family, and as she let me lead, she felt more secure. I had gone from being an irresponsible and self-focused man to being engaged in our relationship. I would do things for her without her prompting and without expecting anything in return, which really spoke her love language. I couldn't believe the conversations I was having with my wife, and it was wonderful. We began growing together spiritually as well, which is probably the most exciting part.

Sure, we had heated moments, but they didn't last like they used to. She began to tell me when something I did bothered her instead of letting it lead to harsh feelings. When we did have a disagreement, I realized this was just our old flesh coming back, and the old "stinkin' thinkin'" was trying to surface. By allowing Christ to live through me, it was easy to give grace and forgive, moving on with our lives.

Our sex life had been lacking. By surrendering our marriage to Him, God brought Mandy and me closer together. I was there for her emotionally like never before, and Mandy responded the same way. This whole process of building our marriage brought a sexual intimacy that we had never experienced. The sex is now back in our marriage, and hallelujah, it is amazing!

As Butch's journey illustrates, providing goes beyond just the paycheck. It also means being an overseer of all the ways of your family and providing for them financially, emotionally, and spiritually. If you defend yourself with the argument that you are doing enough just by providing an income for your wife and that's all you can do, you will eventually face a consequence. You probably won't have the kind of marriage you desire. In other words, if you refuse to invest more in your marriage, you won't have a wife who is willing to be intimate in all the ways God intended—sexually, emotionally, and spiritually. You'll be missing out.

Our society is fine with men finding their worth and purpose in reaching success in the workplace, and success there often translates to a large income. God may lead you to be financially successful, but He may not. Staying on God's path will require prayer, godly friends, your wife's prayers, and constant abiding in Him. Others around you at your workplace and even your boss may not understand when you make your family a priority. God will give you wisdom and strength to make decisions that honor His principles as you trust Him.

Sharing the Journey on the Home Front

After one of the first games played at Carolina Courts, I was impressed with the actions of the teenagers on one of the teams. They cleaned up their bench area, threw away trash, straightened up chairs, and wiped up spilled water. These young men, without being asked, saw that the opposing team left without cleaning up their bench, so they stepped up and took care of the other teams' debris. They weren't thinking about whose job it was to clean the bleachers. They just saw what needed to be done, and they did it. What a great lesson for the teamwork needed in marriage.

Husbands and wives need to develop a system to divide up responsibilities on the home front. After all, someone must manage the "stuff" of your lives—yard work, housework, bills, errands, car repairs, kids' activities, maintenance, and schedules. God wants us to be good stewards of all the material blessings we have, and that means taking care of them.

Much of the assignment of duties in marriage may work itself out naturally, or you may find that you need more discussion about household duties. You can make a list and come to an agreement about who does what. These duties, of course, are not set in stone, but having a general plan helps to keep life somewhat organized and keeps expectations realistic.

Scripture offers two guidelines helpful for sharing the journey on the home front. Galatians 6:5 (NLT) says, "For we are each responsible for our own conduct." This emphasizes individual responsibilities. But verses 2 and 3 emphasize teamwork: "Share each other's burdens, and in this way obey the law of Christ. If you think you are too important to help someone, you are only fooling yourself. You are not that important." How easily we get wrapped up in seeing only our own concerns. God moves us beyond ourselves into consideration of our spouses' needs.

Scott is now the one who works full-time outside the home, and I'm a stay-at-home wife and mother and part-time writer and speaker. Consequently, our roles are fairly traditional. The home duties, such as laundry and cleaning and cooking, are generally mine, while outside duties—garage, yard, and cars—are his. This has evolved naturally through the course of everyday life. Also, we consider one another's natural abilities. I'm pretty laid-back and don't pay attention to details, so I'm not very good at getting the bills paid on time. That's Scott's responsibility. I can't write unless the house is somewhat organized and picked up, so housework is generally my responsibility. That doesn't mean, however, that I do it all. I had to recently remind the three males in my home that we have an incredible modern invention called a dishwasher with only one little drawback—it doesn't load itself, so if they could remember to do that each night with their ice cream dishes, that would just be super.

At times, perhaps because of stress, fatigue, or illness, your wife will need you to step in for her. For example, when I am trying to meet a writing deadline or preparing for an upcoming speaking event, Scott takes over what are routinely considered my responsibilities, and vice versa. I'm not going to ask Scott to move the Christmas decorations from the garage to the attic right now because I know how incredibly hard he's working to get our new business off the ground.

Whether women are full-time homemakers or are employed outside the home, they often feel as if their jobs never end. Women constantly have mental checklists running in their heads. When you step in and help your wife with any of her to-do items, she feels supported and loved by you. Sometimes the littlest acts of help and kindness can make us feel as if we're on the same team.

Many wives I've talked to long for more of a team player on the home front. They say their husbands seem to think their job is done when they walk in the door after work. I've seen evidence of this as I've heard husbands make angry or defensive statements like this: "I'm providing her a great living. What more does she want?" This may be the same husband who wants to be romantic with his wife later that night. Chances are that's not going to work out very well.

Dear husband, your wife wants a partner on her team. If you're not physically home and engaged when you're there, she's not going to feel as if you're supporting her. Remember that your wife is relational by God's design, and she wants to feel connected to you by sharing life's ups and downs. How can you engage with your family when you're home? Try not to bring work home. Avoid being on your cell phone or computer all the time while home. Shoot hoops with your kids or go for a family walk. Make sure your wife and children know they're your priority.

Your wife just feels better about life when you are home. She may not be able to put her finger on the exact reason why she wants you to be home. She just knows that when you're home, she feels a big sigh of relief.

Picture your wife with a huge backpack on—one that is almost bigger than she is. It's stuffed full, and items are even poking out of the half-zipped pockets. Imagine her straining under its weight; imagine how cumbersome it is as she puts away groceries or lifts a child out of the high chair. She sometimes pauses to catch her breath. Now, imagine walking in the door. You go over to her and take off that heavy backpack, and her whole body relaxes with relief. She straightens up and begins to move more easily. She hugs you and goes back to what she was doing, but now her eyes are brighter, and she's smiling. That's how a wife feels when her husband is home and working as his wife's partner.

Sharing the Journey of Parenting

Last night Zachary headed upstairs to watch TV while I went upstairs to read. This left Tyler downstairs with Scott. As I turned to leave, I heard Tyler say to Scott, "So it's just the two of us down here?" I could hear the excitement in his voice as he realized he was going to have his dad all to himself. Nothing warms my heart more than seeing what a great relationship my sons have with their father. I mean that—nothing! Not the best chocolate chip cookie in the world, not a few hours of shopping, and not the best mystery book. If I could pick one thing I want in a husband, it would be for him to be a great father, and I know many women feel the same way. Raising children to be healthy, whole, and godly is important to your wife, and I'm sure it's important to you. Sharing the journey means you are partners in parenting.

When I hear a father say he is babysitting his kids, my head spins. That's not babysitting; it's being a father. Many of us did not grow up with hands-on fathers. If that's your situation, you may need to examine your behavior to see if you've automatically started following your own father's bad example. You can break unhelpful patterns and become the father God wants you to be.

Be United

As I've watched my husband coach kids, I've learned about the power of a team. Scott can take a handful of average athletes, teach them how to pass, how to play their positions, and how to use their individual strengths to help the team—and this team will beat a team of gifted athletes who are ball hogs. The same principle is evident in a united marriage. The synergy of a smoothly functioning team surpasses the strength of its individual parts. As father and mother, one of your greatest strengths is your united purpose. In Mark 3:25, Jesus explains what happens when a household is divided: "If a house is divided against itself, that house will not be able to stand."

How can you practice unity in your daily life? If you disagree with your wife's decision about a parenting issue, wait until you're away from the kids before you talk about it. Don't tell your kids to keep secrets from their mom. If you see your daughter not obeying her mother, make sure she understands that she needs to obey both parents. When your daughter sees you supporting her mother, she will know that she cannot manipulate her parents.

Take time to decide how you will discipline, what the consequences will be, and what values you want to impart to your children. As parents you'll make a million choices, from who's going to read bedtime stories to the preschoolers to who's going to teach the teenager how to drive. When a husband and wife work as a united team, they provide their children with a sense of security.

Scott tells my boys over and over again what a great mom they have. That's one of the best things he does for me! When I hear him say that, I am so encouraged. When Scott's gone, he'll ask the boys on the phone, "Have you told your mom you love her today? Have you thanked her for taking you to practice? Don't ever forget you have the best mom in the world." Consider the way you treat your wife, especially in front of the children. You've probably heard the saying that more is caught than taught; in other words, your children are watching and modeling your behavior, including the way you treat your wife.

A Father's Special Role

A father plays a unique role in the lives of his children. A little girl's first experience of a man's love comes from her father. His love makes her feel special, beautiful, and treasured. If she is secure in her daddy's love, she will be confident as she grows up. She will look for a husband who will treat her with love, respect, and honor, just the way her father treated her mother, and just the way he treated her. Without her father's special love, she might try to fill in the gaps in unhealthy ways.

A father's love for his son teaches him how to be a man. When a father follows the heavenly Father's example, his love shows his sons that a man can be both gentle and strong. Doing "guy" stuff with your son, like playing a video game or throwing a football, will probably be easy for you. But also be involved in the gentler aspects of parenting so your son learns both sides of being a man. Be the one to tuck your child in at night, to say prayers, or to listen as he talks about his day.

Both our sons reached a turning point when they began to gravitate away from me and toward their dad. Now, all they want is to be with their dad, regardless of what he's doing. If he's going on an errand, they want to ride with him. If he's working at the gym, Tyler just wants to be there as Scott's assistant. Zachary wants to stay up till his dad gets home so they can talk about important life matters, such as what's wrong with the Minnesota Timberwolves and why they can't win a game.

Whenever a father spends time with his child, he's adding a drop of glue to their relationship, and eventually that bond is so tight that Dad becomes the one a son turns to for advice or the one a daughter runs to for a hug. The best parenting flows from a love relationship that is built as parents and children spend time together. Children seem to have an incredible sensitivity to sincerity and hypocrisy. Discipline without a solid relationship may work, but it won't be as effective as it is when your kids know you love them. And they know you love them because you tell them every day and because you show them over and over again by the time you spend with them.

Family Priorities

Think about some of the families you know. You probably associate certain words with certain families. For example, when I think of our friends the Vaughans, I think of three active and energetic young girls. I also think of their family as relational. Both Kelly and Phillip love to reach out to other families, and they do this in a variety of ways—leading small groups for other men and women in their neighborhood and community, counseling couples about marriage, and hosting countless guests in and out of their home. Their three daughters have seen their parents model hospitality, servanthood, and Christ's love, and they too are taking on these characteristics.

Every family has its own personality, regardless of whether it was created consciously. Over the course of life you determine your family's personality by purposeful choice or by default. Your values and priorities come to light, and they become a part of your family's personality. Your children's natural bents and interests will also shape your family.

Your family's personality is developed as you live out your priorities as husband and wife. When considering your priorities, think about where you spend your time, money, and energy. Do your actions match your values? Do you need to make any adjustments? If a relationship with the Lord is important to you, you will naturally lead your family to church, you'll have family devotions, and your children will notice you having a quiet time each day. They'll see you live out God's principles.

The word *basketball* is often associated with our family. Scott and his three sisters grew up playing basketball, his dad coached, and his mom attended every game. Basketball remained Scott's love as he got older, so he introduced both our sons to the game. Zachary took to it like white on rice, as we say in the South. Tyler likes sports, but he likes many other things too. He's creative and more inclined to build things, so we make sure our family is not only about basketball. We are sure to make room in our lives for Tyler's love of music (thus the guitar lessons) and his creative bent (thus the Legos in every room of our house).

Family Rhythm

I like life at a steady pace; Scott likes to go full tilt. So we compromise and try to find a rhythm that suits us. We'll have seasons of lots of activity, but then we'll have other seasons that are more laid-back. When Scott was traveling a lot, we learned to prioritize family time when he was home. Now Scott is still away frequently as we get this new business off the ground. That means at least once a month we try to have a family night at home. It's just a time when we four Chitwoods hang out. Maybe we'll watch a movie, shoot hoops in the driveway, or play a board game.

Our rule is to have each son involved in one activity at a time. If we let them take on more than that, life gets out of hand. That's worked for Zachary because his one and only passion is basketball, but Tyler's situation has been different. He's tried lots of other activities—guitar, art, and a variety of sports. Still, when we add something, we also try to take something off the calendar.

We try to have a family meeting at regular intervals—once a week if possible. For us this means looking at the master calendar, the magnetic one on our refrigerator, and making sure we're all on the same page. At our family meeting we can also touch base about what happened during each person's week. One way we do this is by listening to each person's highs and lows. Our kids love this activity, and something about it leads to openness. We don't judge what each person says; we just use the opportunity to talk and to find out more about each other. Sometimes we do this at the dinner table.

A family meeting time can also include a devotion time. As the spiritual leader of your home, consider being the one to initiate this time. You might want to purchase one of many books designed for this purpose. Each family member could memorize the same verse, or you could focus on displaying a particular godly characteristic that week. Perhaps you want to have devotions, but actually having them is challenging. We have had the same experience. I'll tell you the best way we've learned to have spiritual input in our children's lives. I learned it from watching Scott, who does it naturally.

Scott talks to our sons about the spiritual lessons he is learning. It sounds so obvious as I write it, but this one simple concept helps us live out exactly what God wants us to do. Share with your children what you're learning from God. If you're learning that God wants you to be careful about your words, talk to the kids about it. If you're learning to control your temper, talk to your kids about it.

One night Scott was lying on Tyler's bed, and I overheard the sweetest conversation. Scott was apologizing to Tyler for being impatient that day and for responding to the family in a short-tempered manner. Scott explained that patience can sometimes be a challenge for him but that God wants him to be gentle, so he was asking God to work on that in him. That's what spiritual leadership looks like in our family, and it seems to catch the spirit of this directive:

> Write these commandments that I've given you today on your hearts. Get them inside of you and then get them inside your children. Talk about them wherever you are, sitting at home or walking in the street; talk about them from the time you get up in the morning to when you fall into bed at night. Tie them on your hands and foreheads as a reminder; inscribe them on the doorposts of your homes and on your city gates (Deuteronomy 6:6-9 MSG).

God wants a father to live an everyday life of faith so his family can see and hear what God is teaching him. You will provide the best example possible when you build your own life on the firm foundation of Jesus Christ.

Leaving a Legacy

Here's a question you may never have thought about before: What comes to mind when your children think of you? Their thoughts would be very revealing, wouldn't they? One day in early elementary school, Zachary came home with a Mother's Day picture he'd created for me. In the middle was a lovely portrait of me wearing a dress made in my favorite colors of pink and purple. His teacher had told him to add four different words that describe his mom. These were his words: *reading, napping, chocolate chip cookies,* and *laughing.* His words fit me perfectly.

Every day you leave your fingerprints on your kids. Do you want your children to think of you as a dad who worked all the time or a dad who pitched baseballs till it got too dark to see? A dad who stayed at home while the rest of the family went to church or a dad who led the way? A dad who exploded in anger or a dad who was firm yet gentle?

A legacy is something that is handed down. Every day through your words and actions you are developing a legacy that your children will carry in their character. The busyness of life can easily keep you from being purposeful in your parenting. Decide today to leave the legacy you really want—not one dominated by busyness and urgency, but one shaped with purposefulness and prayer.

I like to remember that God is a parent too. So who better to turn to for parenting advice? I also like to remember that God loves my children even more than I do, and He will fill in the gaps for me and Scott as we seek Him first. Regardless of what kind of father you've been, today you can decide to add to and improve the legacy you are leaving. These are the only days we have with our children. We don't get them back. Begin today to be the father you really want to be.

Not Just a Wife

We end this chapter on your journey with your wife by remembering that you and your wife are more than the roles you play as husband and wife, father and mother. These roles are enormously important in life and part of your calling, but you are first a child of God. Ephesians 2:10 (NLT) tells us, "For we are God's masterpiece. He has created us anew in Christ Jesus, so we can do the good things he planned for us long ago." God has assignments for both you and your wife that will bring glory to Him as you become who He created you to be and as you participate in the good things He has planned for you.

Certainly those good things include your roles as husband and wife, and father and mother. Nevertheless, each of you needs to step out of those roles sometimes. You will have to find ways to balance this within your family's rhythm, but if you are seeking God, He will show you how to do this in a way that keeps your family in harmony.

Your wife needs you to remember she's not just a wife, and she's not just a mother. One of the most important acts of love you can show your wife is to encourage her to step out of those roles sometimes. For example, for many years I attended my church's women's retreat. Scott stayed home with the kids, so I knew they were getting great quality time with their dad while I was being refreshed with God and my girlfriends. Being away from all my responsibilities for two and a half days was all I needed to come home revitalized and with a renewed sense of appreciation for my family. (Of course, I had to remind Scott for several years that I would be even more refreshed if the house were clean when I came home. After many discussions, he understood that if I walk into a messy house, I immediately begin my mental to-do list, and all that relaxation I felt is gone in the blink of an eye.)

Allowing your wife to step out of her role as a wife and mother can be as simple as offering to clean the kitchen, encouraging her to go out with a friend, or simply suggesting she go take a nice long bath. These simple acts will refresh your wife as she takes some time to do whatever she wants to do, not what she has to do.

Another key way to share the journey with your wife is to give her support as she explores other interests—her spiritual life, friendships, hobbies, dreams, or career. I've always been in some type of women's Bible study, and I know that I have needed the friendship, wisdom, and support of other women. I'm a better wife and mother because of the wisdom of my godly friends. Scott has always encouraged me to grow in my relationship with the Lord, and consequently, I've been able to become a Christian writer and speaker. Without the sacrifices he's made for me, I wouldn't be able to do what God called me to do.

In the same way, I never want to be the one to keep Scott from pursuing the dreams God has planted in his heart—even if it means becoming gym owners, which I can assure you I never imagined! I wasn't sure how my ministry of speaking and writing would fit into our new plans. I've trusted God that it will all work out, and so far, it has.

Whatever interests your wife; whatever makes her feel alive; whatever makes her think, *This is what God created me to do*, encourage her to do. My brother, Scott, and his wife, Margaret, are great examples of this in the way they support one another's creative bents. Margaret, an actress, explained how much it meant to her that Scott supported her interest:

> The way Scott never thinks I'm silly when I want to try something is so important to me. After 42 years of believing I couldn't sing, I decided I wanted to take singing lessons. Scott never laughed at me, and when I worried I wouldn't be able to sing, he encouraged me to try. I asked him not to tell anyone I was doing this because I wanted to get comfortable with it before I started talking to others. He never told anyone.

I'll end with some of the sweetest words I've ever heard a wife say about her husband. Cris Nole has experienced the kind of love in her marriage that God wants every couple to experience. As you read her words, let them encourage and challenge you to value above all else the journey you share with your wife.

> On a Sunday night, I was asked to share my testimony at one of our local churches. As I looked out into the crowd my eyes locked with my husband's. It was then that I understood that I represented not just myself but my marriage—my husband and the depth of the love he has for me.
>
> I truly represent what it looks like when a husband loves his wife like Christ loved the church. My husband has stood by me, stood with me, and even let me go so that I may grow. He allows me to be broken and has stopped trying to fix me. He loves me unconditionally and has taken on the burden of my past so I can heal in the present. He rejoices in my strengths as well as my weaknesses, and he is who I want to run to when life is good and when it's bad. He has become my biggest encourager, my prayer warrior, and my best friend.

Every time I give my testimony, I find myself falling deeper in love with him. As a result, when you look at me and see my life unfolding before you, know that I don't just represent myself, but rather what Christ intended for a marriage to look like.

PRAYER GUIDE

Heavenly Father,

I am so thankful that I have my wife's companionship as we share life's journey. Sometimes I am too focused on my job, my own interests, my own opinion, and my way of doing things. Help me to keep my focus on You, and then I know my priorities will be what You want them to be. Lord, show me ways my wife and I can be a stronger team. Open my eyes to how I can be her partner on the home front and in parenting. Lord, I pray that my wife will know that she is a masterpiece created for a unique purpose. Let me be an encourager and supporter of her in all the ways You call her to Your purposes. I pray that our marriage will be more united than ever. Lord, put a hedge of protection around our marriage and fortify us with Your strength. Protect us from the attacks of the enemy and let us stand strong so our marriage and our family will bring glory to You. Amen.

8

Kids, Kitchen, and Kissing

~ ෙ ~

As I begin this chapter, I recall the response from some men to my first book, *What a Husband Needs from His Wife*. Many of them jokingly asked, "Where's the chapter about sex?" Well, there wasn't a sex chapter, although I certainly addressed that topic throughout the book. This book, however, does have a chapter about sex. That may seem ironic considering the input Scott gave me about the topic of sex. When I asked him what I should tell wives about a husband's needs in this area, he responded with something I've heard him say frequently: "Any sex is good sex. Just tell them to have sex. Lots of it. That's all." That would have made for a very short chapter, so maybe that's why I didn't include it in my book for wives.

Though I begin this chapter in a lighthearted manner, I have approached the content prayerfully. Many couples experience so much contention in the area of sexual intimacy that it ends up tearing them apart rather than enhancing their oneness. We live in a sex-saturated culture, where distortions and warped thinking about sexual intimacy run rampant. So as always, let's counteract the lies with God's Word.

Let's look again at the very first marriage. Genesis 2:24 reminds us that God made Adam and Eve "one flesh." In other words, He ordained their sexual intimacy. This is His big stamp of approval of sex within the context of marriage, and it prohibits it outside of marriage (see also Exodus 20:14). Sex is to be great fun and to be enjoyed by both spouses. If we look at just a few verses in Song of Solomon, a beautiful love story of King Solomon and his wife, we immediately see that this couple is reveling in the physical aspect of their relationship. In Song of Solomon 7:1-3, the king praises his wife:

> How beautiful are your feet in sandals, O prince's daughter! The curves of your hips are like jewels, the work of the hands of an artist. Your navel is like a round goblet which never lacks mixed wine; your belly is like a heap of wheat fenced about with lilies. Your two breasts are like two fawns, twins of a gazelle.

This couple is having a great time with each other! And I think that's exactly what God wants. God could have created sex for just one thing—procreation—and that's obviously one of its purposes. It could have been just a mechanical, physical act. But God didn't stop there. God, the giver of all good gifts, designed sex to bring great pleasure to married couples.

The marital bed is to be a place where a husband and wife enjoy the journey of knowing each other. Genesis 2:25 explains that "the man and his wife were both naked and were not ashamed." God designed marital intimacy to be the closest, most open, and most vulnerable experience a couple can have. It's a way to offer your entire selves to one another. It can be a risky journey, and that's why we find this kind of intimacy only in the security of a permanent and committed marriage.

We know that sex can be great, but we also know that sexual issues can be divisive. That can be hard to understand. If marital sex has God's stamp of approval, shouldn't all our dreams come true in the bedroom?

One of Scott's comments about husbands in general helps to explain this: "We men are not that complicated. Just keep it simple." I hope that doesn't offend you, for it's not intended to. Scott said it when we were discussing some issues and trying to come to a resolution. As I think about this statement, it seems to be a key for sexual intimacy. For men, sexual intimacy is simple and straightforward, but for women, it's a little more complicated. Let's look at some of the differences between men and women in the area of sexual intimacy. Will you pray right now to grow in your understanding of your wife's needs in the area of sexual intimacy?

Great Expectations

One of my main dreams growing up was to get married, have children, and live happily ever after. At the age of 27, living in Atlanta, Georgia, and working as a high school English teacher, I'd already celebrated with most of my best friends as they got married. I was beginning to wonder if I'd ever meet my prince charming. And then my principal hired a young man from Minnesota to teach math. Scott was (and still is!) cute, friendly, and down-to-earth, and we quickly fell in love.

One year later we were married in my hometown of North Palm Beach, Florida, with hundreds of friends and family in attendance. My fairy-tale wedding day is still one of my happiest memories. I wore a billowy, white Cinderella dress and loved feeling like a princess for a day. My groom was handsome and charming. As we laughed and celebrated on our wedding day, I thanked God for making my dreams come true.

The wedding night, however, was not what either of us was

expecting. As we arrived at our hotel room, both of us were looking forward to the night ahead! Within a few minutes, however, I noticed loud music coming from outside. Looking out the window, I saw an outdoor concert taking place. I immediately decided I could not spend my wedding night at that hotel with the loud music blaring all night.

"Honey, we cannot stay here. We have to go find another hotel."

Scott looked at me like I was an alien, but he calmly replied, "It will be fine. We won't even notice the music after a while."

I was not convinced. I started packing up our bags and announced, "I will not stay here. Either you get the car or I will."

We then proceeded to have one of the biggest fights we'd ever had. I was crying, and we were both screaming.

The night went from bad to worse. We left the hotel in stubborn silence and drove to another hotel about ten minutes away. Unlike the luxurious hotel room we had reserved, this new hotel was budget all the way. The air conditioner was not yet running, so when we got into the room on the night of July 6 in south Florida, the room temperature was close to 100 degrees. I turned on the air conditioner and fell onto the bed in complete misery.

Then, in an attempt to move things toward romance, Scott suggested we use the hot tub in our room. All I could think was, *Sure, getting hotter than I already am sounds like so much fun.* However, I also wanted to try to save our sabotaged night. I turned on the hot tub and couldn't believe what happened next. The water jets were not pointing down in the tub as they should have been. Instead, they were pointing up, directly toward our bed. The water completely soaked the bed's comforter and sheets.

Finally, all we could do was laugh. No, it was not quite the wedding night we'd expected.

To say that we both had unfulfilled expectations that night would be an understatement. I'd planned my wedding day and night down to the last detail, and I was expecting it to be perfect. I'm sure Scott's expectations did not include exiting a hotel room on our wedding night.

Throughout marriage, some expectations are met, but some aren't. Picture those expectations as a suitcase. The suitcase is crammed so full that you can hardly pull it. The heavy suitcase of our marital expectations can make marriage much more difficult than it needs to be. In addition, husbands' and wives' expectations are often different from one another's. Counselor Dan Ascher offers a helpful explanation:

> Husbands and wives each have valid needs in marriage. For example, it's okay for a husband to want his wife to be adventuresome in the bedroom. It's okay for a wife to desire to go out on a monthly date with her husband. Neither need is wrong. What's important is what we do with these needs. Do we look at these needs as desires or as expectations? If we look at our needs as desires, we'll talk to God and to our spouses about these desires in marriage. On the other hand, expectations bring a sense of entitlement: I have the right to do this, and I don't care what you think.

Dan explains that we need to go to God with our sexual desires, talk to Him in prayer, and ask Him to meet our desires through our marriage partners. We also need to talk specifically with our mates about our desires and work on making sexual intimacy fulfilling for both husband and wife.

Husbands and wives probably have greater expectations about sexual intimacy than about any other aspect of marriage. Those hopes have been called "sexpectations," and they are rarely the same for husbands and wives. Let's look at what a wife needs from her husband in the area of sexual intimacy.

What Turns Her On?

Here's a scenario I found common to many women I talked to. Your wife is unloading dishes from the dishwasher, talking to you as you're eating cereal at the breakfast table. She bends over to retrieve dishes, turns to put them on the shelf…and next thing she knows, her husband is offering to "unload her dishwasher," and his suggestive tone and playful actions make it clear what he's talking about. Granted, I love the idea that sex begins in the kitchen, but this is not what most women have in mind when they hear that. Men are generally more visually stimulated than women, thus explaining the dishwasher scenario, but your wife probably responds differently. She can be physically attracted to you without being sexually stimulated.

So what *does* make your wife interested in sex with you? Women are more open to sexual intimacy when they have been loved emotionally. Just as a man has been wired a certain way, created in God's own image, this is how a woman has been created. You'll notice that this chapter is about two-thirds of the way through the book. That placement is intentional. When you love your wife in all the nonsexual ways we've discussed in this book, you will make a worthwhile investment that will increase your intimacy, including your sexual intimacy.

Remember that becoming one flesh is about intimacy. It's about the lifelong journey we take with our spouses as we get to know one another. In our everyday language, we use all sorts of words and phrases for sexual intimacy. I like to think about the difference between the connotations of the words *have sex* and *make love*. The second phrase describes what God was truly after when He created a married couple to be one flesh—knowing each other physically, emotionally, mentally, and spiritually.

One of the Bible's key directives to husbands is Ephesians 5:25. Earlier I referred to the rendering in The Message: "Husbands, go all out in your love for your wives, exactly as Christ did for the church—a love marked by giving, not getting." Your wife will generally look for an emotional connection before she wants to connect with you physically. Are you going all out in loving your wife emotionally? Are you going all out in loving her the way she needs to be loved? Look back at the previous chapters. Take a mental inventory and ask God to show you ways you can continue to go all out in your love for your wife.

One wife told me, "I need him to romance me before sex—long before—not just as we get into bed." Your wife needs you to touch her heart so she will be ready to respond to you sexually. Kevin Leman explains this in his book *Sheet Music:*

> A man is wise to make love to his wife outside the bedroom. What does that mean? It means he's a helper. He helps with homework; he tucks the kids into bed. He takes the family's turn in the carpool; he drives the kids to their practices. He's a good daddy; he's an attentive husband. He listens to his wife talk about her day, because he knows it's important to her and because they share one heart. He uses his authority to protect, serve, and pleasure his wife...If a woman feels treasured by her husband, she'll be more than willing to meet him between the sheets. And if a husband is sexually fulfilled, he'll take a bullet for his wife. That's love. That's sacrifice. And that's what marriage is all about.[1]

Hand-Holding and Hugs

Along with an emotional connection, affection is important to a woman. In other words, sometimes she wants you to touch her without it leading to sex. "Hold me with no expectations of *anything* else happening," said one wife about her need for some cuddling. Affection communicates sincere, genuine love to a woman. For a woman, affection goes hand in hand with love. She is likely to think, *If you love me, why on earth wouldn't you hug me or hold my hand?*

What are some ways to show your wife affection? Hold her hand, put your arm around her as you sit by her or walk with her, snuggle with her. If you pass by her, just reach out and touch her and massage her shoulders. Kiss her just to kiss her, not to lead to more. Make these non-sexual ways of touching a habit in your relationship with your wife.

A wife is tuned in to her husband's sincerity and motives. If you touch your wife only when you want it to lead to the bedroom, she may feel used. She might feel as if you're only interested in getting your own needs met. Your motives may not be that selfish—your desire is to connect with your wife, and sex might be the most natural way for you to do so. But God's love asks you to move beyond yourself, to show a mature love, a love that does not seek its own (1 Corinthians 13:5).

One wife told me she feels as if her husband truly doesn't see her until he wants to have sex with her. She went on to say she feels he knows nothing about her, nothing about what she thinks or feels, and he doesn't seem to want to. He doesn't ask about her job or what happened with the kids that day. She said he just checks out until he wants to have sex. She explained that because of this, she feels used, not loved.

Much of my time with Scott these days is spent at Carolina Courts, as he's working really long days. When I get to the gym, he stops what he's doing to give me quick greeting and kiss. He'll usually take time to sit by me, and maybe we'll have a few minutes to catch up or to watch our sons play a game. He holds my hand or puts his arm around me, and these simple gestures mean so much to me. He's honoring what's important to me by giving me his time and affection.

What's one specific habit you can develop in this area today? Greet each other with a hug and kiss when she comes home, snuggle while you're watching TV, and hold your wife's hand as you walk in a store or take a walk. Try it today, and remember to expect nothing in return.

Appreciate Your Wife's Beauty

A woman absolutely must feel good about herself physically to be responsive sexually. Otherwise, she might have difficulty feeling sexy and being interested in sexual intimacy with her husband. Even when a woman knows that society's ideals of beauty are unrealistic, resisting the temptation to compare herself to this ideal is nearly impossible. She is constantly wondering if she is sexy enough, young enough, and skinny enough.

Our culture can also shape a man's thoughts of beauty and give him unrealistic expectations. Gary Thomas explains, "The day I was married, I began praying, 'Lord, help me to define beauty by Lisa's body. Shape my desires so that I am attracted only to her.'"[2] Consider praying a similar prayer for your marriage. Also, if anything in your life is contributing to an unrealistic view of beauty, get rid of it.

God calls you to love your wife by rejoicing exclusively in her beauty. That means you don't let your eyes stray to a woman walking by in short shorts. That means you don't even comment to your guy friends that another woman is hot. It means you're careful about where your eyes go. If movies tempt you to lust after someone other than your wife, even a fantasy, then don't go there. Same with TV images or computer images. I know from talking and corresponding with many women that most women struggle with insecurity about their appearance. You, dear husband, are one of the few people who can help your wife to feel beautiful. When you look at other women, your wife feels her beauty diminished.

Husband, you cannot tell your wife frequently enough how beautiful she is to you. Tell her she's beautiful, and show her with your tender actions. Katie wrote about how loved she feels when her husband tells her specifically how she is beautiful to him:

> I love it when my husband says that he has a favorite part of my body. I recently found out that my least favorite part—and it's very easy for me to list what I consider my flaws—is his favorite part. While it could be of a sexual nature, it doesn't have to be. My husband has told me before how beautiful my neck and jaw line are when I pull my hair back. It made me feel so special!

Mental and Physical Adjustment

Remember our previous discussion about the way men can compartmentalize easily? Men have a work box, a hobby box, a wife box, a kid box, and so on, and they can hop into the sex box very readily. Ginny said, "Guys can be having a stinkin' awful day, but there's nothing to stop them from having great sex. In fact, sex will be the cure for that awful day, a horrible fight, or feeling stressed out." You can probably relate!

Women, on the other hand, need more time to adjust mentally to be ready for sexual intimacy and more time physically to experience fulfilling lovemaking. Women don't generally compartmentalize as readily as men do, so they need time mentally and physically to disengage from all the other aspects of their lives. Amy said, "I can't go from Mary Poppins to Pamela Anderson in 30 seconds flat."

How can you help your wife adjust so she will be ready for sexual intimacy? One way is to create a mood that helps your wife disconnect from everything else. Consider the five senses for setting a romantic mood. Light some candles, play music, massage her feet or shoulders, and allow time for soaking in a bathtub. Especially when your children are young, make sure your wife has a little bit of alone time at the end of the day.

The title of this chapter, "Kids, Kitchen, and Kissing," might seem like a strange combination, but this is its origin. We have some friends who created a routine that we thought was a great idea. After dinner, one spouse cleans up the kitchen, and one gets the kids bathed and tucked in. This allows the wife to have some alone time, thus helping her make a mental adjustment. She might read a book, take a bath, take a walk, or just enjoy not being in the mommy role. Try this in your own household. Let your wife have some time to mentally shift from responsibilities to lovemaking. It helps her mind turn off all other cares and tune into you.

Sometimes your wife will not be ready to be physically intimate unless she's had time to talk to you about something that offended her. Hurt feelings can be a big barrier to physical intimacy. We're told in James 5:16, "Confess your sins to one another, and pray for one another so that you may be healed." Honest conversation and sincere apologies can help you to become more intimate in all ways.

Another way to help your wife mentally adjust is to get her away from distractions and responsibilities for an extended period of time. A weekend getaway might be what you both need to ignite your sex life. When away from your daily responsibilities, you can focus on your relationship in a way that you can't otherwise. Make room in your budget for this. If money is an issue, be creative—can you borrow a friend's lake house or mountain house? Can the kids spend the night with someone while you enjoy being home alone? One of my favorite getaways was only half an hour away. We can drive from the suburbs to uptown Charlotte just for one night away. If you do the planning, your wife will really be delighted. Don't forget to arrange care for the kids, pets, and home. Let your wife truly be free from responsibilities so you can focus on each other.

Art TerKeurst recounts how getaways have helped his marriage:

> Lysa and I slipped out of town for three days. We went to a bed-and-breakfast in the mountains, a place that was a female five-senses home run. There was no TV (so Sportscenter was out of the question), but for Lysa this place was as if she had been whisked away into a woman's wonderworld weekend. For three days I witnessed a transformation in my wife—she didn't have to worry about poopy diapears, dirty dishes, and deadlines, and she entered a state of complete softness and relaxation. You'd think after one day the place would get a little old, but it never happened. She felt the way you and I would feel if we were sitting in a new Triton 19-foot bass boat for three days on Lake Okeechobee. Or maybe playing 18 holes with Tiger Woods at Augusta National the day before the Masters. This wonder-world weekend softened Lysa's senses and called forth her femininity, of which I was the happy recipient.[3]

Just as your wife needs time mentally to adjust to sexual intimacy, her body also needs more time than yours does. Men are generally more quickly aroused physically and more quickly satisfied than women. "Most researchers indicate that even under the most favorable conditions and when highly motivated, the average wife requires ten to fifteen minutes or more to reach orgasm."[4] One wife told me, "Men sometimes need to think about nonsexual things, like baseball, to slow themselves down. On the other hand, I'm trying to get my thoughts in the moment. It's hard to for me to think about what's going on right now because I have so many other thoughts going on. If I can get my mental attitude right, it's great, and I really enjoy sex." Most women will agree that if they have time to mentally adjust and to physically get aroused, they will be willing and sexually responsive partners to their husbands' desire.

Seek to Please Your Wife

Read The Message version of 1 Corinthians 7:2-5:

> It's good for a man to have a wife, and for a woman to have a husband. Sexual drives are strong, but marriage is strong enough to contain them and provide for a balanced and fulfilling sexual life in a world of sexual disorder. The marriage bed must be a place of mutuality—the husband seeking to satisfy his wife, the wife seeking to satisfy her husband. Marriage is not a place to "stand up for your rights." Marriage is a decision to serve the other, whether in bed or out.

I love the last two sentences here because they zoom in on what needs to be a priority in all aspects of marriage, including sexual intimacy: the importance of serving your spouse. You can serve your wife in the marriage bed by learning what pleases her sexually. If you're not sure what pleases her or how her body works, find out! Don't be shy about reading books, such as the ones I cited in this chapter. Have conversations about how to please one another sexually.

Learning to please your wife sexually might sound intimidating, but rest assured, this doesn't mean you have to be a perfect lover to please your wife. As in all aspects of your marriage, what's important is not that you follow steps x, y, and z. What's more important than perfect performance is your heart. Above all else, sexual intimacy is about the loving relationship you have with your spouse. Let your physical intimacy truly be an expression of love. Consider her needs in and out of the bedroom, and you both will benefit.

What Comes First

It's easy to get caught in the "what comes first" rut. The husband usually wants sex first, and the wife usually wants emotional connection first. But husbands and wives need to be careful of having negative assumptions about each other. *All he thinks about is sex,* a wife might think. Likewise, a husband might say to himself, *I have to jump through so many hoops just to have sex with my wife!* The truth is probably somewhere in the middle.

Love always expects the best of the other person. A husband's need to have sex is not just about the physical. It's also about wanting to connect with his wife, and this is the road he takes. In fact, it's usually the most natural route for a husband. That doesn't mean he's wrong or that his wife is wrong for wanting to connect other ways. When a husband and wife get beyond feeling angry or frustrated by their differences, the truth is that they love each other and want to please each other. A good sex life is just as important as a good emotional connection, and marriage is a journey of discovering how to love each other the way both people need to be loved. "When you improve your marriage, you'll usually improve your sex life. When you improve your sex life, you'll usually improve the rest of your marriage. The two are intricately entwined, so making more effort in any one area is a very good investment."[5]

Hormones Make a Difference

Speaking of physical differences brings us to an important topic that affects our sex lives: hormones. We are physical beings, created by God with various hormones that affect our sex drive. Men's sex drive is generally higher and more constant due to the hormone testosterone. This hormone tends to be much more constant and stable than a woman's hormones.

A woman is affected by hormones as well. A woman's body is designed to bear a child, and God gave her unique hormones to enable her to do that. About two weeks into her 28-day cycle, at ovulation, she will experience an increase in estrogen and testosterone. Both of these hormones may increase her libido, and physically this makes sense as this is the time when she is most likely to be able to conceive. Many women say that they also feel more sexual during their menstrual cycle. Because of the ebb and flow of their hormones, women's sexual drive will not be as consistent as men's. Husbands and wives need to learn how these hormones affect sexual intimacy.

Hormones may also alter your wife's general disposition or mood, which in turn can affect her desire to be physically intimate. Premenstrual syndrome, or PMS, has both physical and emotional symptoms. If your wife is PMS-y, she might be easily irritated, down, and overly emotional. She may have headaches, increased fatigue, and painful menstrual cramps. Most women experience at least some of these symptoms, and while they're not an excuse for ungodly behavior, they are very real. I've heard many jokes about what PMS stands for, such as "Pack My Suitcase," "Provide Me with Sweets," or even more severe, "Pass My Shotgun." These jokes may be funny, but the truth is that hormones are real. Don't dismiss the effect they have on your wife.

Over the course of marriage, you will learn how hormones affect sexual intimacy. Your wife's hormones may call for an extra measure of understanding from you. At the same time, hormones cannot be used as an excuse for not being sexually intimate. Sex is a vital part of marriage, and this is an area of your marriage that you need to work on so it will thrive and so you will be satisfied with each other. Like any difference in your marriage, differences in sexual intimacy can be worked out as you both seek the Lord and both seek to please each other.

Guarding and Protecting Your Marriage

One evening many years ago while Scott was gone flying, I called him during dinner. We chatted for a while, and then I asked, "Who are you having dinner with?" It really was just a conversational question, not premeditated at all, but this question soon became a weighty matter.

He answered, "A flight attendant."

"Oh, you went with the flight crew?" I asked, knowing they would often eat together.

"No, it's just me and a flight attendant."

"Oh." Long pause. "Let's talk later."

He called me immediately upon returning to his hotel room, knowing this was a situation we needed to discuss. He had not invited the flight attendant to go with him; she had invited herself. Scott said it had happened quickly, and he just responded in his normal, friendly manner. I wasn't happy, but I understood how that situation could happen. I completely trust Scott. It's one of the best parts of our marriage and really a gift considering how many years he traveled with his job. Nevertheless, I also know that none of us is immune to temptation. I know how he can appear to another woman. He is friendly and talkative, and if a woman doesn't have those qualities in her own husband, they can be awfully appealing in another man. I also know that many nights alone in a hotel room can present temptations. After our discussion, Scott readily agreed that out of respect for me, he wouldn't go out to dinner with just one other woman. The next time this situation came up, he explained that he needed to go with a group.

A wise couple will build a wall of protection around their marriage. The sexual purity of godly marriages is under constant assault. A married couple needs preventive plans in place and "heat of the moment" plans as well. They need to realize that regardless of how great their marriage is, it is a spiritual battlefield. Satan's attack on marriage began long ago as the serpent whispered lies and Eve and Adam took the bait (Genesis 3). Satan will try to make you think your spouse is the enemy. He'll create discord and isolation, making you more vulnerable to sexual temptation. One of you might struggle with lust or pornography. One of you might even have an affair. The enemy uses sexual sin as a doorway into your marriage.

Let's look at several ways you can guard and protect your marriage.

Build Trust

Some of the bricks comprising a protective wall around your marriage are bricks of trust. Trust is essential in any good relationship and especially in your marriage. You establish trust in all the little ways you demonstrate your commitment to your wife and family. If you say you're going to be home at a certain time, are you? If you commit to going to your daughter's dance recital, are you there? Can your wife trust you to be faithful to her with your eyes and actions? You develop trust as you practice integrity by living by God's standards in all areas of your life.

Another way to develop trust is by being truthful. Remember who is called the father of lies? Satan. Lying is sin. Are you keeping any secrets from your wife? Is there anything about your life you don't want your wife to find out about? Maybe you have a friendly relationship with a woman at work that your wife doesn't know about, or you've downplayed the significance of this friendship. Are you open with your wife about e-mails and text messages? Couples must establish their own boundaries in this area of technology, but I wonder, if you don't want your wife to have access to your e-mails, why not?

Have the difficult conversations. Talk to your wife if you're struggling with lust or some other temptation. Talk to a trusted godly male friend. God wants you to bring it to the light. These conversations are not easy, but until you are honest, you will not have freedom.

Trust builds a sense of security, which is a vital need for your wife. She will trust you when she's sure your heart has no room for any other woman. Rachel Olsen, speaker and writer for Proverbs 31 Ministries, explains how this works in her marriage:

> My husband is a professor at a state college in a beach town. He goes off to work each day surrounded by barely dressed, attractive, intelligent twenty-year-olds. Yet I feel no need to question his fidelity. Rick has set boundaries and established routines that everyone can see, and they help to shield him from temptation. I also know him to be trustworthy and a man of integrity. Even if his allegiance to me isn't particularly strong on a given day, I trust that his allegiance to God is.

Watch Your Thoughts

I've often heard a story about the best way to boil a frog—not something I can imagine needing to know, but it offers a good lesson. The story goes that if you put a frog in a pot of boiling water, his survival instincts will immediately detect the danger, and he'll quickly jump out. On the other hand, if you put a frog in a pot of cool water and gradually turn the heat up, he won't recognize the threat until too late. The lesson for marriage is to be aware of gradual temperature increases. Sin doesn't usually start with an obvious, blatantly immoral situation. Rather, temptation comes little by little, and we eventually find ourselves in a place we never intended to be, dealing with temptations and sins that have become almost more than we can bear.

I've heard people say that an affair just happened. That's not really an accurate portrayal of what happens between two people who've become attracted to one another. A more accurate description would be to say that the attraction happens little by little and thought by thought. It starts with a friendly conversation with a workmate, a soulful look into another woman's eyes, and a few flirtatious comments. From there you may start having thoughts about this other woman, but they seem innocuous or even innocent. Perhaps you find yourself wondering if the other woman finds you attractive, or perhaps you look forward to your next conversation with her. These thoughts about a woman other than your wife are dangerous because they can lead to unfaithful actions.

Watch Your Eyes

God's standards for purity are far different from the world's ideas. Concerning the sin of lust, we've all heard comments like these: "There's no harm in looking." "It's a guy thing; women just don't understand." I agree that most women don't understand how easily men are visually stimulated. However, I don't agree that looking is harmless. The husband who lets his eyes linger on a woman other than his wife is hurting her, even if she doesn't say anything. It's a hard thing to talk about, and maybe she doesn't want to stir up your anger by sharing her true feelings. Rest assured, however, your wife will be hurt and your marriage will suffer if you do not practice faithfulness with your eyes. God's standard is clear in Matthew 5:27-28: "You have heard that it was said, 'You shall not commit adultery'; but I say to you that everyone who looks at a woman with lust for her has already committed adultery with her in his heart."

Take an honest look at yourself to see if you need to spend time in confession with the Lord and take steps to change your sexual behavior.

Jesus goes on to say that this is an area where you need to go to an extreme: "If your right eye makes you stumble, tear it out and throw it from you; for it is better for you to lose one of the parts of your body, than for your whole body to be thrown into hell. If your right hand makes you stumble, cut it off and throw it from you; for it is better for you to lose one of the parts of your body, than for your whole body to go into hell" (verses 29-30). Whatever tempts you—magazines, movies, the Internet—avoid it. I know of a Christian speaker who travels almost every weekend and stays in hotel rooms, which normally have TVs, privacy, and access to X-rated movies. He knows this temptation is not one he wants to battle, so he requests hotel rooms with no TV or with blocked channels. This is an example of Jesus' command to "tear it out and throw it from you."

Establish Boundaries

Take time after reading this chapter to agree with your wife on certain boundaries for your marriage. You may already have unspoken guidelines, but the sexual purity of your marriage is so vital that you need to protect it by taking time to have a discussion. Here are three boundary options you might want to consider.

1. No one-on-one time with a woman other than your wife. Obviously, your work, ministry, or other activities may put you in situations where you are alone with a woman. Even in these situations, however, you can guard yourself from temptation. For example, you can leave your office door open when meeting with a woman. When you're working with a woman, you can limit the time you're with her or even include other coworkers.

2. Do not have a friendship with another woman. Friendship is an intimacy that should be reserved for your wife. Period. Of course, you will be friendly with other women, but being friendly is not the same as enjoying a friendship. Remember that a woman's attraction to a man often starts with an emotional connection, so a friendship is very attractive to her. In fact, a woman may easily misinterpret your friendliness. Also, be careful about reaching out in friendship to a woman by means of e-mails, text messages, or phone calls. Don't confide in one another, especially about your marriages. Even if you're not sharing anything with another woman, be careful not to let another woman confide in you.

Be careful about your friendships with other couples as well. If you are blessed with good couple friends, be thankful because finding a couple you both enjoy can be difficult. Appreciate their friendship as a couple, but don't spend time one-on-one with the other wife.

3. Be careful whom you talk to about your wife and how you talk about her. Your words to others about your wife should cover her privacy, her weaknesses, and her secrets. Your aim should always be to present her in the best light. How would your wife feel if she overheard your words about her?

Maybe you can't imagine being tempted by another woman or taking a relationship further. That's something to thank God for, but still, every couple would be wise to acknowledge that no one is immune to temptation. Just because you can't imagine it doesn't mean you don't need to be cautious. Remember that relationships develop little by little. Little by little the time you spend with the other woman might increase; you might have more and more personal conversations. A friendship with another woman can soon replace the emotional intimacy you should have with your wife. This type of intimacy might lead to a touch, a caress, a kiss, or even more. If this happens, you're shaking the foundations of your marriage. Let's be honest. It's easy to be attracted to someone you don't live with day in and day out, someone you never see at her worst, the way you do your wife. That kind of relationship is a counterfeit. More importantly, God wants you to reserve intimacy of all types for your wife alone.

Truthfully, when I was married only a short time, I probably would have thought these boundaries were pretty extreme, so if you're thinking that, I understand. However, after many years of marriage, along with speaking and writing about marriage, I have seen way too many Christian marriages fall apart because couples failed to have safeguards. They didn't take preventive measures to guard their marriages, and this contributed to their downfall.

Enjoy Your Wife

I'll end on a positive note and remind you of where we started. Proverbs 5:17-20 (MSG) says, "Your spring water is for you and you only, not to be passed around among strangers. Bless your fresh-flowing fountain! Enjoy the wife you married as a young man! Lovely as an angel, beautiful as a rose—don't ever quit taking delight in her body. Never take her love for granted!" I love the words "Enjoy the wife you married as a young man." Marriage is the only relationship where we can speak the language of sexual intimacy. God wants sex to be a good gift, one that both of you enjoy and that draws you closer to each other.

PRAYER GUIDE

Lord,

Thank You for the gift of sexual intimacy. I pray that our lovemaking will be something we both enjoy and that it will create greater intimacy in our lives. Show me, Lord, how to love my wife the way she needs to be loved. Then make me willing to serve her in all ways, including in our marriage bed. May we have desire only for one another, and may our sexual intimacy satisfy both of us.

I especially pray that You will protect both of us from sexual temptation. Help us both to keep our marriage bed undefiled in thought, word, and action. Protect us from the attacks of the enemy, and do not let sex be an area that gives the enemy a foothold into our marriage. Where we need honest communication or confession, Lord, let us have the humility and courage to do what needs to be done. Amen.

9

For Better or for Worse

As you stood at the altar on your wedding day watching your beautiful bride walk down the aisle, I'm sure your heart was filled with many emotions: happiness, excitement, awe, and maybe some fear and trembling. You recited your vows and looked forward to the good times ahead:

> I, _____, take you, _____, to be my
> wife; to have and to hold, from this day forward; for better,
> for worse; for richer, for poorer; in sickness and in health;
> to love and to cherish; till death do us part; and hereto I
> pledge you my faithfulness.

At moments like that, most of us think only about the happiness we're going to share in marriage, not the "worse" or "poorer" times we refer to in our vows. Because of this, we can be disillusioned by the hard work marriage sometimes demands. Our expectations for marriage can be like a young boy's expectations of Christmas morning. Just when it seems all the presents have been opened, his parents present him with one final box. He grabs the wrapped box, certain it contains the one thing he's been hoping for. The box is the right shape, it's wrapped perfectly, and his parents always save the best present for last. He tears off the paper, digs into the box, and pulls out...a remote-control car, not the Nintendo DS he'd expected. He smiles and says thank you, but he can barely hide his disappointment.

Don't we do the same thing with marriage? When the brightly wrapped gift of marriage doesn't turn out to be quite what we hoped for, not as easy or carefree as we had imagined, we try to hide our disappointment as we scramble to hang on to our marital bliss. Perhaps we would be wiser to focus on how to deal with the hardship before us.

If I could give any advice to engaged or newly married couples, it would be this: Expect hard times. They may start with simple daily stress, and they can include calamity. Rest assured—the hard times will come. I don't want to sound like a pessimist, because I believe God wants us to rejoice in our marriages, but Scripture makes it abundantly clear that a child of God will experience hardship and not the continual ease and comfort we so often associate with happiness.

Christ Himself suffered, and countless men and women of faith in the Bible suffered. I think of Joseph, Job, Jeremiah, and Jesus Himself. Paul lists many of his trials in 2 Corinthians 11:22-32. Look at the way Peter teaches us to face hardships: "Beloved, do not be surprised at the fiery ordeal among you, which comes upon you for your testing, as though some strange thing were happening to you; but to the degree that you share the sufferings of Christ, keep on rejoicing" (1 Peter 4:12-13).

The storm that blows through your marriage can be a drizzle, a good soaking, a downpour with thunder and lightning, or a hurricane. It can pummel your marriage with everyday stress or a major crisis: job issues, parenting concerns, financial pressures, sickness, broken promises, conflicting dreams, loss or change, addictions, or infidelity. In this chapter we'll hear the stories of several couples' hardships. You may not experience the same challenging situations, but these couples' stories will provide principles that will help you turn toward God and toward your wife during tough times.

Many of the couples I have interviewed repeated a noteworthy statement. They agreed that their marriage was better after getting through the hardship than it had been before the storm. May their stories give you the same kind of hope for your marriage.

Turn Toward God

Scott's journey to become a pilot was a long one—working full-time as a school teacher and coach while going to flight school part time, then becoming a flight instructor, then working as a pilot for a small airline, and finally landing his dream job with a major airline. He had worked a little less than two years for US Airways by the morning of 9/11. Scott knew this day would have an enormous impact on the airline industry, and sure enough, by December of that same year, Scott was laid off from his flying job. After pursuing this career for ten years, he faced the stress of losing his income and the heartbreak of losing his dream.

Scott and I were both filled with disappointment as we saw our dreams turn to dust. Both of us had spent years making sacrifices and working diligently to reach our goals. Scott had always wanted to be a commercial pilot, and I had always wanted to be a stay-at-home mother. I knew that I might have to go back to work, and Scott knew that flying jobs would be scarce with so many other pilots in the industry facing unemployment as well. We both wondered, *God, why did You let us have this dream for such a short time? What does our future look like? Will Scott have to leave flying? Will we have to move?*

I read several Scriptures during that time that helped me take my eyes off our uncertain circumstances and focus on the Lord. I wrote them out and posted them in our kitchen to remind us where our focus needed to be—on Jesus Christ, not on our circumstances.

Trust in God's Purposes

One of the verses I displayed in our home was Mark 8:29. Jesus asks Peter a penetrating question: "Who do you say that I am?" God seemed to be asking Scott and me, *Who do you say that I am during this hard time? You've declared your trust in Me during the good times. Will you continue to trust Me when you are facing uncertainty?* In the account in Mark's Gospel, Peter answered Jesus, "You are the Christ." In the same way, we affirmed our faith as we learned to pray, *You are our Lord, and we trust You even when life is not working out the way we had hoped.*

Hopelessness, fear, worry, weariness, anger, and bitterness can easily overtake us if we focus on our trying situations. However, if we focus our minds and hearts on the Lord (see Hebrews 12:1-2), our perspective will shift from an earthly one to a heavenly one. With the lenses of faith, we see that our trials help us to mature. Our faith will become firmly based on God and not on circumstances that provide temporary ease or comfort. Our faith will declare, *Lord, I'm not sure where this is going, but I'm sure of You.*

A heavenly perspective affirms that God is sovereign and holds the plans of our lives in His hands. Of course, I'm writing this with hindsight, but I love to trace God's fingerprints in past events to see how they led to our family owning a business. I truly believe that if Scott had continued with US Airways and earned a larger salary each year, he would not have walked away from that career. Six months after his furlough from US Airways, he became a corporate pilot and earned a more moderate salary. Also, his new schedule gave him more time at home, which was a big plus in many ways for our family. He was able to coach our sons' basketball teams and get more involved in our community sports association.

That's where Scott met Ron Esser. They became good friends, they discovered they shared a similar vision for youth sports, and Ron eventually suggested opening an indoor basketball facility together. I love knowing that God has orchestrated all the events leading to the place where we now are. You can have that same assurance in your marriage whether storms are brewing or the sun is shining.

Turn Toward Each Other

During Scott's layoff from US Airways, he searched full-time for a new job, and I appreciated how hard he worked at it. He closed himself behind the doors of our home office, where I wouldn't see him for hours. At the end of each day, after tucking our two sons into bed, we'd sit on the couch (usually with a bowl of ice cream), and he'd recount what was going on with the job search. I looked forward to this time together so I could be included in his efforts.

I talked to pastor Ron Hilliard, associate pastor of North Palm Beach Presbyterian Church, whose marriage is an excellent model and who has counseled numerous couples in crisis situations. He points out the importance of communication before and during a hard time:

> One of the main problems I see in couples is that they often stop communicating in the middle of the hardship. They shut each other off or out, and they feel as if the other person doesn't understand them or even try to understand them. Couples stop listening or stop seeking to understand what's going on with the other person. Learning to listen and taking the time to listen is really important. It's important that you learn to do this first when your marriage is not under pressure. When you're not investing in your marriage in the good times, you're not going to do it in the difficult times. So establishing a regular pattern of communicating and checking in with each other

emotionally is a key foundation for getting through any future difficult times.

I appreciated so much the way Scott communicated with me by keeping me informed about any possible job leads. He let me know when he was feeling hopeful or discouraged and what he needed me to pray for. I never felt I was in the dark, left to guess, or forced to imagine the worst about his job search. We both had fears, of course, but we worked hard not to let our fears or worries separate us.

Living in the city of Charlotte, which has a large banking industry, we know many couples who have lost or are uncertain about their jobs. I've heard some of these women talk about how important it is that their husbands let them know what's going on, even if the husbands say only that they really don't know anything. Many wives say they can handle anything as long as they're not shut out. As a husband who is committed to his wife, honor your wife's need for connection during hard times, just as you do during the other seasons of your marriage.

Any marriage hardship presents us with a choice: We can turn toward one another or away from one another. In other words, we can let the struggle make us stronger as a couple, or we can allow the challenge to tear us apart. Good communication is an essential in marriage that can keep you turning toward one another during a storm.

Don't Give Up

What's one of the biggest issues couples fight about? Money. If you're like most couples, financial matters have added some conflict to your marriage.

Writers Curt and Marybeth Whalen have written an honest and practical book called *Learning to Live Financially Free* in which they share how they've learned to face their finances without conflict. In a story adapted from their book, Curt shares honestly about this journey in their marriage.

One of the most difficult things Marybeth and I are learning as husband and wife is how to communicate about our finances. When we were first married, we realized right away that our views of handling money were very different. Marybeth was a saver who wanted a rainy-day fund, but I had grown up spending all I made on music, clothes, and going out with friends. Also, I was the nerd who wanted to talk through all the intricate details of my spreadsheet. Marybeth tended to get overwhelmed with my formulas and calculations. Instead of working together as a team as God intended, our budget meetings ended up in fights with each of us retreating to our respective corners.

I'm ashamed of the way I blew off her opinion about how to handle money. I took care of the day-to-day transactions—writing the bills, balancing the checkbook, and so on—so I disregarded her suggestions whether they had merit or not. I was prideful, stubborn, controlling, and downright disrespectful to her.

After living for years with these kinds of communication problems, our financial situation became desperate. We were tens of thousands of dollars in credit card, car loan, student loan, and IRS debt. We were treading water trying to stay afloat, but the weight of our financial problems began pulling our marriage under. We were drowning in debt, miles apart emotionally, and ready to give up.

Fortunately for us, our Heavenly Father loves to give second chances.

One cold December night four years ago, Marybeth and I sat in our car in a Walmart parking lot and had a conversation that changed our lives. As we watched people hurry to and from the store, we talked about our fears and frustrations from the past. After years of fighting and blaming each other, we realized that the only way out of our mess was to work to fix it together. We discovered a common vision of what our family's finances could become and decided to do whatever it took to become financially free. God sat with us that night in the car, wrapped His arms around our shoulders, and helped us take the first step towards healing our marriage.

Marybeth and I had to learn two key principles in order to have honest communication about money. First, we had to agree that there was no "yours" and "mine" when it came to our family's finances. The money from my paycheck belonged to both of us equally. We couldn't have separate checking accounts or bills that "her" money paid and bills that "my" money paid. We had to unite and work as a team in order to create a solid, biblically based financial foundation to conquer our money problems.

Even more important, I had to learn to become more accountable to Marybeth for what I spent money on, and to realize that she had an equal vote in the budget decisions. I had to listen to her, really listen, and learn to value her advice. I had to quit writing off her ideas as silly or stupid just because I wasn't the one who came up with them.

Over time, God slowly chipped away at the stubbornness that surrounded my heart and opened my eyes to the stupid and selfish way that I was leading my family. I began to realize how disrespectful and unloving I had been to Marybeth. God was slowly opening my eyes to the wisdom of her advice.

And now, after four years, we've paid off nearly a hundred thousand dollars of debt, we have begun building up a full emergency fund, and we have calm discussions about budgets, the cost of college, and retirement. After years of working against each other, things for Team Whalen are looking up.[1]

I appreciate the Whalens' honesty about how learning to be on the same financial team took time and persistence in their marriage. They had to try to understand each other and commit to finding common ground. One of the most revealing aspects of Curt's story is his humility. He admits his mistakes, and that has been a huge part of their victory in this area. If you're struggling with simply living within a budget or facing insurmountable debt, I encourage you to read their book and learn from their experiences.

Another aspect of their story that stands out is that their financial situation was an ongoing issue with no quick or easy solution. Marriage requires our commitment to one another and our perseverance. Did you notice how much debt the Whalens paid off? Nearly $100,000! Their financial struggles provide an illustration of James 1:2-3: "Consider it all joy, my brethren, when you encounter various trials, knowing that the testing of your faith produces endurance. And let endurance have its perfect result, so that you may be perfect and complete, lacking in nothing." The word that stands out to me in these verses is *endurance*. Their struggle didn't end quickly or easily. They experienced defeats and victories, but they persevered and reaped the benefits because of their commitment.

I also want to highlight the attitude James encourages us to have during hardships. We're to "consider it all joy." God wants us to rejoice, praise Him, and even thank Him for trials. That's a challenge. That means thanking God even when we don't necessarily feel joyful. We don't necessarily thank Him *for* the specific trial but rather *in* the trial. Praise is an act of trust, saying, *We trust You, God. We trust Your purposes, and we trust that You are good all the time.*

Accept the Way Your Spouse Handles Stress

Illness is another hardship a couple may face. Chris and Dean Hogan experienced a hardship when their third child was born with a life-threatening illness. The Hogans learned that they respond to stress differently from one another. A very trying time became even more stressful as they misunderstood one another's reactions to the crisis. Chris shares their story:

> I was 25 and pregnant with our third child. Dean and I were excited about adding to our family. We already had two healthy children and prayed for another healthy baby. We rejoiced when our youngest was born and appeared healthy after I had four long months on bed rest. Unfortunately, we were back in the hospital in a week. By the time our baby was five weeks old, he was being scheduled for life-saving surgery with a diagnosis of a rare and often deadly liver disease. He survived surgery and cardiac arrests. Only five days after surgery, the doctors told us to take him home with an overwhelming schedule of medications to administer. We would just have to wait and see.
>
> Dean and I were left with a mix of emotions and stress to deal with. What we didn't realize is how differently we handle stress. Dean is forever the optimist. I am the realist, researching and analyzing every fact available to arrive at a logical conclusion. Dean accused me of always seeing the glass as half empty. I was falling apart inside, knowing the gravity of the situation, while Dean continued to say our baby would be fine.
>
> We argued constantly. I would yell at him, "Wake up! Our baby is going to die! We have to start dealing with it!" The stress of caring for a child with critical health problems plus two preschoolers was more than I could handle. Dean tried to help caring for the kids while still focusing on his job—a job he could now not afford to lose with the needs of a sick child.
>
> Dean and I leaned on God and prayed constantly together through this time of extreme faith and growth. But the stress proceeded to pile on top of us. Fortunately, I had a wonderful mentor encouraging and challenging me. She said, "God

can restore your marriage, and we are going to start praying for it to happen right now." From that day on, Dean and I started to pray for God to restore our marriage.

We resurrected date nights. We made a conscious effort to spend quality time together. Dean and I became honest with each other about our stress and how we were feeling. After several long months, we became best friends again. The feelings of love and attraction came back.

Dean and I now know how the other person is going to react during a crisis and afterward. I understand when Dean seems slow to grasp the reality of the situation. I'm now thankful for his optimism instead of finding it annoying! He understands I will look straight at the facts the same way the doctors do. He also knows I will be calm during the crisis. I may seem to be handling it all in stride, but I'll crash and burn a week later. We know when to give each other space and when to hold on tight.

Most importantly, Dean and I discovered firsthand that God is good regardless of what happens in our lives. His faithfulness is revealed in a tangible way during our times of crisis. God gives us grace and love for one another when a crisis comes along.

The Hogans reached a huge milestone when they learned to accept each other's unique responses to stress. We can easily judge rather than accept or understand, but God wants our differences to bring strength to our marriages rather than create disunity. As Chris and Dean learned to accept each other's unique personality styles, they were able to turn toward each other for support.

Amazing Grace

Brooke and Russ have a great marriage. They laugh a lot, they text and call each other throughout the day, and their love and affection for one another is evident. When I told them I wanted to talk to them about their marriage for input for my book, I never imagined the story they were about to share with me. I expected to hear about some of the strong aspects of their marriage, but they shared honestly and authentically about their struggles. I am thankful to them for their transparency. Although I've changed their names and some details of their situation to protect their privacy, they and the other couples mentioned in this chapter are available for correspondence through my e-mail address. Brooke begins:

> Russ worked in the restaurant business, 70-80 hours a week, and I also worked full-time. We were living what people would describe as the good life—beautiful house and cars, money in the bank, nice things, and two healthy children. We also had a really good marriage. Even though we both worked a lot, we talked frequently on the phone. When Russ was home, he was very involved in our marriage and family. He was a great husband and dad. If you had asked me then, I would have said we had a great marriage.
>
> One Friday night, Russ was sitting on the bed while I was getting ready for our date night, and he was acting odd. He seemed to be in a fog. I could tell something was up, so I asked him what was wrong. He said, "I need to talk to somebody." I said, "Okay, babe. Let's talk. I'm here."
>
> He said, "I can't talk to you about this." Now I knew something was really wrong because we talked to each other about everything. I immediately called a dear friend from church, and she contacted our pastors. One of the pastors called Russ, and they talked privately for a long time. I still didn't know what was going on. The next day, Russ met with this pastor, and when he came home from the meeting, he said, "We need to talk."
>
> I never could have imagined what Russ told me: He had lost his job, and he was addicted to cocaine. He had a

daily habit. He had completely wiped out all our money. We were close to losing all that we had—our home, our cars, everything. He also told me that during the meeting with our pastor, he had prayed to give his life to Christ. He told me over and over again that he was very sorry and that he loved me. He said he understood that I might want to leave him or never forgive him. He had finally gotten to the point where he couldn't hide his addiction anymore and he couldn't continue to lie to me.

I was numb at first, but then every emotion flooded over me the next few days. *Why? Where? How?* I screamed at him. I was filled with hate, and I was devastated. Within a few days, my survival instinct kicked in. I decided he was not going to be in my life or my children's lives. I thought to myself, *He chose this path, and I'm not going down with him.* We had no money. Every single penny was gone.

Russ explained some of the factors leading to this point in their lives:

> I felt so much pressure all the time. To continue our lifestyle, I had to work constantly, and to do that I had to have more energy. From the first time I tried cocaine, it seemed like the answer. It also gave me an escape from the constant feelings of pressure. I believed the lie that it would fix things. Of course, the more I used, the more I needed. But when I told Brooke the truth, I was finished. I couldn't do it anymore. From the day I gave my life to Christ, I never touched drugs again.
>
> I felt as if the weight of the world fell off my shoulders. I started reading God's Word constantly, and I met with accountability partners every day. A few weeks after praying to receive Christ, I was baptized, and that first breath I took after coming up from the water was just incredible.

Everything looked bright, including people's faces and the future. I left my addiction in the baptism pool.

Brooke continued their story with emotion in her voice and tears flooding her eyes.

I hated him, and I was disgusted by him. I felt so betrayed, and my hatred consumed me. I turned away from God. I kept asking God, *Why did You let this happen?* At first I confided in only one good friend from church. She never judged Russ or our marriage. She just pointed me to Jesus.

At this point I was just trying to figure out how I could leave Russ and how I could survive with two kids on my own. Russ and I continued going to church, and we were even in a small group—studying the topic of marriage, of all things! Russ joined our church's softball team. I never went to watch him, but when my kids begged me one day, I went. At this game something totally unexpected happened, and I can see now that God used it to help me consider not leaving Russ.

During the softball game, Russ stepped in a hole and broke his leg in three places. He had to be in complete traction for six weeks. He could not move at all or do anything for himself. I really couldn't believe this had happened. I said to God, *I hate this man, and now You're going to ask me to wait on him hand and foot?* It seemed like too much. I was broken.

When we were in the hospital, my cell phone didn't stop ringing with calls from friends from church. God's grace started falling down on us—meals, money, gift cards, food cards, gas cards. Many were from friends, and many arrived anonymously. People were helping with the kids and with Russ. This outpouring of love completely blew me away. As these people surrounded us, I knew God was saying, *Look—they're not judging him or judging your marriage.* Little by little I began to open up my heart—just a tiny bit—toward Russ.

I knew God was asking me to serve my husband as if I were serving Him. After getting home from work, I would walk up the stairs and pray, *I'm serving You. God, that's You in the bed, and I'm going to ask You what You want to eat.* This was the only way I could do it.

Meanwhile, Russ was writing out Scriptures for me, praying aloud, and writing notes telling me how much he loved and appreciated me. Although I had been blinded by hurt and shut off by such a feeling of betrayal, I began to consider staying together. As I saw the changes in Russ, little by little God began to soften my heart.

We have worked on our own relationships with the Lord, and we have worked on our marriage. Sometimes I'm not even sure how we did it. I just know God did it. God provided. We still have our house. Russ has a job in a different business. We still have our marriage. Our kids are great kids. After a year had passed, I could truly say that our marriage was better than it had been before.

What took place in Russ and Brooke's marriage to make it better than ever, even in the light of a tremendous challenge? Let's look at some practical lessons from their experience.

Keep turning to God. "Prayer was the key to rebuilding our relationship. We prayed constantly, individually and together. We also turned to God's Word and read it together," Russ and Brooke agreed.

Pour out your heart to God. Tell Him everything, even the ugly emotions. If you read Psalms, you'll see the psalmists express every emotion imaginable. God can handle all our emotions and thoughts. You don't have to clean yourself up or put on an act before God. He sees all that happens in your life, He forgives you when you confess your sins to Him, and He loves you unconditionally.

Turn to others, especially other believers. During a marriage crisis, you need a good support network of friends who will encourage and challenge you. You need friends who want your marriage to stay together, who will offer you godly counsel rather than bad-mouth or blame the offending partner. In certain situations, you may also need to respect your spouse's need for privacy. One spouse may want to share freely while the other spouse wants to be more cautious. Respect each other's confidences, but at the same time, don't keep the sin hidden. Bring it to the light, even if that means confiding in one other person. Let that one person hold you accountable to God's standards.

Allow trust to be rebuilt. Brooke said that only after much time and prayer could she trust that Russ's heart really had changed. She needed to be sure he wasn't just saying or doing things out of his desperation to hold his family together. "I needed him really to do what he said he was going to do. I needed proof. I needed to see that I could count on him." And Russ didn't get defensive or impatient with Brooke. He kept his focus on the Lord and allowed Christ to heal their marriage over time.

Be honest with each other. "Certain things will trigger memories or hurt from that time. We talk about what we think and feel. We don't let things build up or become bigger issues than they should be. Honesty is so important. We are learning to say things that we know the other person would rather not hear." Brooke and Russ agreed that their communication is better now than it had been before and that this has been a key in their healing.

Brooke ended our talk with an amazing declaration:

> I'm thankful for what we went through. I wouldn't go back and change anything. If I knew then that it would bring us to where we are now, I would have thought, *Bring it on. Do anything you need to, God.* When I tell people this story, they just can't believe it, and sometimes they say they don't think they could have survived. I want couples to know they

don't need to say that. When you need God's strength and grace, you'll have it. Not before, but right when you need it. Even now as I tell our story, it's sometimes hard for me to believe that this really happened to us. That's grace.

If you are feeling hopeless about your situation, listen to Brooke's words. God's amazing grace will cover you during a crisis. You will have just what you need when you need it—as long as you keep turning to God. I'm not underestimating the turmoil of a crisis in a marriage. I understand very well how incredibly difficult staying together can be. However, I also know that if these couples had not faced their challenges with the mind-set that marriage is a permanent commitment, they may have not made it.

On the other hand, if you have been through a divorce, know that God loves you, He's seen your pain, and "there is now no condemnation for those who are in Christ Jesus" (Romans 8:1).

Storms from Within the Marriage

Maybe you think you could survive a storm that comes from an outside force, such as job loss, financial troubles, trouble with a child, or life-threatening illness. But what about a crisis in your marriage that a spouse has caused? What if a spouse's infidelity is the cause of the storm? Could you survive this storm?

A crisis that is caused by you or your wife will shake the love, trust, and security you have built in your marriage up to this point. You may be overwhelmed with rage and pain. You may think you could not possibly stay in your marriage.

I want to share with you a story about a Christian couple whose marriage was rocked by infidelity. I hope you are never in this situation, but please don't skip this section just because you think it has no relevance to your marriage. This story contains some lessons that will help prevent your marriage from ever getting to this point. Also, you may know another couple who needs this information. I'm so thank-ful for this couple's willingness to share this story, and I hope their honesty will help any marriage threatened by the same storm. This is a true story, but I've changed the names and some details to protect everyone's privacy.

Erica discovered one morning that she had left her purse in her husband's, Pete's, car. She called him and said she'd come get it from him at work. She drove to his workplace, got her purse from the car, and decided to go in and say hello to Pete and possibly have lunch. When she got to his office, she learned he was in a meeting, so she sat at his desk and began to surf the net while waiting. As she opened up his computer screen, she noticed an instant message that had been minimized. She opened it up and was shocked by what she read: a flir-tatious, friendly, intimate message from one of Pete's female coworkers. She began to open up other messages and e-mails, only to discover that Pete and his coworker were obviously very involved and intimate with one another.

To say she was shocked and devastated is an understatement. She was shaking, crying, and sick, all while sitting at her husband's work-place. When Pete walked in the office, he knew Erica had discovered his secret emotional affair with a coworker. After they left the office, Pete confessed that the relationship had been going on for some time, that they had not had sex, but they had been physically intimate in other ways. He had violated their marriage vows.

I asked Pete how their marriage got to the point where this was a temptation and then a choice for him.

> Looking back, I can see how we got to this point. We moved to a new city for my job, and we knew no one there. I was working all the time, so Erica and I soon became very dis-connected. We quickly lost our close friendship. We either were fighting or yelling at one another, or we were just iso-lated from one another, doing our own thing. Our lives

revolved around our child, but beyond that we didn't really have a good marriage. I didn't feel appreciated, and I really needed that. I felt building resentment and just got to the point where I didn't care about Erica's feelings.

Things were awful at home but so much easier at work. I worked with Renee and enjoyed her company. Her admiration and respect for my work were attractive to me. I began to believe the lie that Erica would be better off without me and that I would be happier with someone else.

The day Erica discovered Pete's emotional infidelity, Pete moved out to an apartment. He explains that Erica was highly emotional, and he knew from past experience that she needed time to calm down. They ended up being separated for approximately two months. Pete says that during this time, he was miserable. He realized that the grass was not greener on the other side, and he really didn't want his marriage to end. Gradually he began to reach out to his wife, and he discovered, little by little, that she too was willing to try to make their marriage work.

Erica asked him to leave his job so he would no longer be around Renee, and Pete agreed. This was a huge step for them. It proved to Erica that Pete really was willing to take drastic steps to get back together.

What can we learn from Erica's and Pete's experience? These guidelines will help you if you are facing an emotional or physical affair, and better yet, they can help you and your wife avoid being in this position.

Make couple time a priority. Erica shared that going away for a weekend to talk was extremely helpful. Pete agreed to answer any questions she wanted to ask because neither of them wanted her to be haunted by her imagination—which proved to be much worse than what had actually occurred. They had no computers, no phones, and no BlackBerries—no distractions and no temptations. They realized they had not been taking time to do this, and their relationship had suffered as a result.

Erica and Pete emphasized the importance of communicating daily. Erica explains how communication comes into play:

> If your wife mentions that something you are doing is giving her cause for concern, don't dismiss it or get defensive. Discuss it, and if you are having trouble, admit it. Nipping any suspicion in the bud keeps down any walls Satan will try to erect again. I'm overwhelmed by God's work in our marriage when I see Pete's loving, remorseful response to my fears about something I feel is inappropriate behavior. We discuss the matter, and nine times out of ten, Pete will not even be aware of how a woman might perceive his actions. He actually thanks me for pointing it out!

Separate from the temptation. I appreciate the way Pete walked away from his job, the place of his temptation. You may need to take a drastic step to avoid temptation. You may need to acknowledge that you cannot necessarily do what other men do, as Pete explains:

> I have new rules in our marriage. I lost some of my rights because I violated my wife's trust. I am very careful about how I talk to other women. Even in a sales call, I'm careful to remain professional and not overly friendly as I would have been before. I work out of my home, so I use the speaker phone so my wife can hear my calls. Erica has free access to all my technology. There are no secrets.

Fortify your marriage with prayer. Prayer for your wife and marriage is so vital. It is the strongest weapon you have to create a protective wall around your marriage. God's Word says that you and your wife have a much greater strength as you invite God to be an essential part of your marriage. "A cord of three strands is not quickly torn apart" (Ecclesiastes 4:12).

Practice forgiveness. If your wife has violated your marriage vows, you must seek to forgive her if you want to move forward in your marriage. God commands us to forgive and will give us His power to forgive. "Remember, the Lord forgave you, so you must forgive others. Above all, clothe yourselves with love, which binds us all together in perfect harmony" (Colossians 3:13-14 NLT). If you've been hurt, you probably won't feel like forgiving, but you can choose to forgive in obedience to God. Trust Him to bring forgiveness and reconciliation to your marriage. That's what Erica did.

> Forgiveness is not forgetting the sin, but forgiving the sinner. You harm yourself when you don't forgive. You may find you have to forgive your spouse on a daily basis for the same offense. Be encouraged as your wife demonstrates her love and new commitment to you and the marriage. Over time, you'll find it easier and easier to forgive. God has shown me that I was not totally innocent, as I wanted to be, in the deterioration of our marriage. My unloving and disrespectful actions toward Pete over the years were fuel to the fire Satan was building.

Practice confession. If you are the offending spouse, be sure to confess your sins not only to your spouse but also to the Lord. He sees your heart and is "faithful and righteous to forgive us our sins and to cleanse us from all unrighteousness" (1 John 1:9).

Find a Christian counselor. This means a counselor who refers to God's Word and shows you how to apply God's truth to your marriage. Your pastor might be a counselor, or he can refer you to someone. You may even have to try more than one before you find someone who can help both of you.

I discussed in chapter 7 some other boundaries in the area of sexual temptation. You might want to revisit that chapter now. I also suggested that you and your wife have a conversation about boundaries in your marriage. If you haven't had that conversation yet, have it now.

Using the Storms to God's Glory

God uses the storms in our lives, including storms in our marriages, to shape our character and to fortify our faith. The couples I interviewed used their trials to make their marriages better, not bitter. They are living proof that "God causes all things to work together for good to those who love God, to those who are called according to His purpose" (Romans 8:28).

I'll end with a reminder that God knows exactly what hardship you face now or will face in the future. Keep turning to Him, knowing that He understands. Some of the sweetest words in all of Scripture are found in Hebrews 4:16: "Therefore let us draw near with confidence to the throne of grace, so that we may receive mercy and find grace to help in time of need." When your path is uncertain and your circumstances are stormy, you can be sure of this: Christ loves you and will always be there for you. He is faithful and trustworthy and will never leave you or forsake you (see Hebrews 13:5).

PRAYER GUIDE

Lord,

We know we will face storms in our marriage. I pray that the storms will draw us together and not divide us. I pray that in any hardships, challenges, or stress that we face individually or as a couple, we will come out the other side closer to one another and closer to You. Help us not to be anxious or fearful during a storm. Instead, let us stand firmly on our Rock, with You, Lord, as our firm foundation. Let us have peace that passes human understanding as we draw on Your supernatural strength. We know that you can bring good out of horrible situations.

I especially pray that You will protect both of us from sexual temptation. Help us both to honor our marriage by remaining faithful to our vows, to You, and to one another.

Give us the grace to forgive when we transgress against one another. We know that because You have forgiven us, we can forgive each other. I pray in Jesus' name. Amen.

10

The Treasure of a Wife

On a crisp and cool spring morning, I joined other family members to watch my twin sister perform a Herculean feat: She ran the Boston Marathon. Several years later I'm still amazed, probably because I've never run more than a few miles at one time. Also, this was her first marathon—at the ripe old age of 40!

As we gathered to watch her run, the energy of the crowd propelled the runners off the starting line. We yelled and cheered for my sister as if we were crazy people, and we shouted and clapped for others as well. Then we gathered our belongings and hurried to the next vantage point to repeat our rooting escapades.

As the race began, many of the runners wore long-sleeve running shirts and pants to protect them from the chill. As the race progressed and their bodies warmed, however, those layers would become hindrances rather than helps, so the runners peeled them off and tossed them to the ground, never to see those items again. In the same way, as we've explored what your wife needs from you, I've asked you to toss aside any attitudes or actions that would hinder your marriage.

After stripping off those extra layers of clothing, the runners were clothed in only lightweight, breathable, moisture-wicking material—fabrics carefully chosen to help them run as efficiently as possible. Likewise, after tossing aside anything that hinders your marriage, you can choose to clothe yourself only in those thoughts and behaviors that help your marriage.

As you think about your marriage race, what unneeded clothing have you tossed aside? What new practices have you adopted that help your marriage? Have you become more attuned to loving your wife the way she needs to be loved? Do you understand more about her needs? Have you become the kind of listener, lover, and friend she needs? I hope you can say you've changed as a result of adopting God's principles for your marriage. We're each a work in progress, and the transformation of your marriage doesn't end when you finish this book. The holy ground of marriage will always be a place of learning to love one another and meet each other's needs.

As I think about running, I think about Hebrews 12:1-2, where we're exhorted to "run with endurance the race that is set before us, fixing our eyes on Jesus, the author and perfector of faith." Rest assured that Jesus is watching you and cheering you on to be the man He wants you to be and the husband your wife needs. He will provide all that you need to love your wife for Him.

Before we end, I'd like to give you my husband's perspective of the marriage race. He wrote what follows on the next several pages.

A Word from My Husband

This is Scott Chitwood, Melanie's husband. To be brutally honest, in 18 years of being married to Melanie, I have screwed up a million times.

As a former airline and corporate pilot, I'll try to explain this in a way that makes sense to me. Pilots spend a lot of time in the cockpit monitoring systems, navigation, and weather. We frequently go to recurrent training to study techniques for quickly dealing with emergencies. As a linear thinker and a guy, I wish marriage could be like that, but that's just not going to happen. I was stubborn for too many years trying to treat it like that.

Marriage is more like the weather aspect of flying. Pilots have to be able to interpret and navigate through and around weather. In my early years of flying, I flew turboprops for a commuter up and down the east coast and in the Midwest. Flying turboprops was a lot of fun, but one thing you learn quickly about turboprops is that they fly at altitudes where all the weather is. I spent four years flying at altitudes that required a lot of navigation through icing and thunderstorms. When I approached a thunderstorm, I had to make some quick decisions.

Obviously, I always wanted to avoid being anywhere near a storm in the first place, but sometimes the scenario would not allow for that. So I had to make a decision: Do I go around it, navigate through it, or turn around and go back the way I came?

This might sound a little crazy, but I loved the challenge of dealing with weather. I loved being able to look at the radar, talk to air traffic control, and look at the weather itself to find a way to get through it. We often tightened our seatbelts to endure a bumpy ride. Most of all, I loved being able to navigate through weather and come out the other side. After a bumpy ride, we would suddenly pop out into calm, stable air, and we would enjoy smooth sailing for the rest of the trip. Occasionally we would look back at the weather we just flew through and see a rainbow.

Navigating a marriage is a lot like navigating the weather. You have to make decisions about how to work with different scenarios, ride out the bumps, and then enjoy the smooth ride that comes with the rest of the trip. Maybe that sounds cheesy, but I feel as if God has given me many experiences that can teach me about being a better husband for Melanie. Are you able to look at experiences you have had and apply them to your marriage?

I spent my last five years of flying in Learjets, which are known for their speed and high ceiling. The great thing about flying at high altitudes is that 95 percent of the time, you are able to fly above any bad weather. When you are enjoying a smooth ride at 45,000 feet and seeing a bunch of nasty weather below you, you feel bad for all the pilots and passengers who aren't able to fly over it.

I want my marriage to be like that Learjet flying at 45,000 feet. I want a nice smooth ride, not a bumpy ride through all the bad weather. Am I there yet? Absolutely not! Will I ever get there? I sure hope so. The key for me is to lay it all down before God. When I was flying, I knew that I had to be at my best for the safety of my crew and passengers. I could not be halfway committed to flying if I wanted to avoid accidents. The same is true in my marriage—I can't be halfway into marriage. For too many years I brought my "A game" to the cockpit to be the best pilot I could be, but I was not bringing my "A game" to my marriage.

Melanie talked earlier in this chapter about running a marathon and how the runners stripped away layers of unneeded clothing. I had a lot of layers to peel away before I could truly say I was ready to be at the top of my game for God and Melanie. As I've run the race of marriage, I've been able to throw off pride and selfishness, the two biggies for me and probably for a lot of men.

Melanie has mentioned my dream of building a basketball facility. For Melanie to completely trust me and support me in this venture has required incredible unselfishness. Melanie peeled away a lot of her layers long ago, and our marriage is much stronger as a result. We're both committed to letting God peel away those extra layers we no longer need. Discarding those things has not always been easy, but the benefits to our marriage have been worth it.

In Conclusion...

Thank you for joining me in this journey of discovering what your wife needs. I prayed for you, your wife, and your marriage even before this book found its way to you. I believe God will richly bless you and your marriage because of the investment you've made in your marriage by reading this book and practicing God's principles.

It's been a journey for me too, causing me to seek God first in my life as I've relied on Him while writing this book and practicing His ways in my own marriage. There's nothing like writing a marriage book to hold you accountable to godly principles in your own marriage. I hope you too have learned to seek Him first, to rely on His wisdom, grace, and strength to love your wife. One of my prayers for you has been that through this journey you will have discovered two gifts. First, I hope you've discovered the richness of a closer relationship with the Lord. Second, I hope you've learned to treasure your wife more than ever.

I recently talked with two of our good friends about their marriage. Julie's husband, Kelly, told her something I hope you can also say about your wife. "Kelly recently told me that he loves me more and more as time passes, and that he is still so in love with me."

When I think about the gift of marriage, I am reminded how gracious God is. He knows our strengths and weaknesses and mercifully provides us with a relationship in which we can count on one other person to be with us throughout our lives. I can sense God whispering, *I have a good plan for your life, and this marriage is part of it. This wife, whom you've committed to, is the one who will help you through life. She'll be the one to listen, to care, to laugh with, to embrace, and to grow old with. She'll be the one to know you like no other person on earth. As you love her and she loves you, you'll get a taste of My love for you, and you'll see a reflection of the intimacy I want to have with you. Embrace this wife as a priceless treasure. Appreciate this priceless gift I've given you.*

I hope the end of this book finds you treasuring anew the gift of the wife God has given you. May you be able to echo Proverbs 18:22: "He who finds a wife finds a good thing and obtains favor from the LORD."

PRAYER GUIDE

Lord,

Thank You for the treasures of my wife and my marriage. Thank You for the transformation You're working in my heart and my actions. Continue to give me the desire and strength to run the race of marriage in a way that pleases You. As I seek You first in my life, may I be the man You want me to be and the husband my wife needs. For all the good, ordinary, and hard times my wife and I have been through, Lord, thank You. I know they're all a part of what You've used to shape us and mold us. We know that You have a good future for us [Jeremiah 29:11] and that You will be the One to hold us together [Colossians 1:17]. When others see our marriage, Lord, I pray that we will shine brightly for You. As the world sees our covenant love, may they be filled with hope and encouragement for their marriages too. Amen.

Study Guide

Chapter 1—The Starting Point

1. Before you continue to read this book, consider making these commitments:

   - I will pursue God. I will spend time every day praising Him, confessing my sins, thanking Him for His blessings, and praying for Him to reveal the truth to me.

   - I will take an honest look at myself and assess the way I have been acting.

   - I will find out what God says in Scripture about marriage.

   - I will apply the lessons God reveals to me in this book.

   - I will pray daily for my wife and our marriage.

   _____

   Signature   *Date*

2. Tell your wife something that is going to make her really happy: Tell her you're reading this book. She might give you a hug or a sweet smile, but she might respond with a sarcastic remark or skeptical look. Don't let her response deter you in any way. Just smile and tell her you love her. Follow through on your commitment to God to pursue His principles in your marriage regardless of the obstacles you face.

3. "The king's heart is like channels of water in the hand of the LORD; He turns it wherever He wishes" (Proverbs 21:1). In what ways does this verse apply to your marriage? In what ways does God want you to turn your heart to Him, to your wife, and to your marriage?

4. What does surrendering your marriage to God mean to you?

5. I write this in chapter 1: "The marriage God wants for you will develop from the transformation of your heart." Look up the following verses and write down whatever you learn about the heart.

   Deuteronomy 4:29

   Deuteronomy 6:25

   Deuteronomy 8:2

   1 Samuel 16:7

   Matthew 6:21

6. What can you relate to in the story of Butch and Mandy Ferguson's marriage? In the story about Gary and Norma Smalley?

7. Do you value your wife as your helper? In what ways does she complement you?

8. Which of your character traits are helpful to your marriage? Which traits hinder your marriage?

9. Read the following statement from this chapter. "Oneness is one of the treasures of marriage but also one of its challenges. We long for intimacy, but it doesn't necessarily come easily. Oneness requires both husband and wife to lay down their rights, entitlement, freedom, independence, and expectations." What is your response to this statement?

10. Will you consider doing something that might seem a little strange? Right now, in light of what I wrote about the holy ground of marriage, will you physically take off your shoes? Stand right where you are and pray, *God, let me have Your perspective of my marriage, a perspective that says that marriage is holy ground.* Feel free to add your own prayers.

11. Reread the section entitled "Assess Your Own Marriage." Identify which of the statements or descriptions you can most readily relate to. If none apply, write a statement that reflects your thoughts and feelings about your marriage.

Chapter 2—Be the Man

1. Read Matthew 6:33. Does your life show that you are seeking God's kingdom above all else? List two examples to support your answer.

2. Read 1 John 4:10. When did Christ first find a home in your heart?

If you're not sure you have a relationship with the Lord, would you like to pray now to ask Jesus to be your Lord and Savior?

3. List in order at least five of your top priorities. Does the investment of your time, energy, and money reflect your priorities? Do you think these are the priorities God wants you to have?

4. Do you have a daily quiet time? What practical steps can you follow to make sure you are having a quiet time?

5. Do you have at least one guy friend who encourages you in your walk with God? Who encourages you in your marriage?

6. Why is abiding in Christ vital to your marriage? See John 15:1-8.

7. Name three ways you can be the spiritual leader in your marriage.

8. If you've never prayed aloud with your wife, start today. Your prayers don't have to be long or eloquent. Just speak from your heart to the One who loves you and desires to hear from you.

9. Read Mark 10:43-45. What lifestyle does Jesus model for you?

10. In chapter 2 I write, "When she is assured your heart belongs to God, you can be assured her heart belongs to you." Is your wife assured that your heart belongs to God? If you're not sure, now might be the right time to ask her.

11. Respond to this statement from chapter 2: "Over and over again as I write this book and reflect on my own marriage, I see that the number one tool God has used to develop my character and mature my faith has been my marriage."

12. Review the commitment statement you signed at the beginning of this study guide. How are you doing?

Chapter 3—Love Her No Matter What

1. Read Ephesians 5:25-33. Are you going all out in your love for your wife? What keeps you from going all out in your love?

2. Romans 5:5 explains, "The love of God has been poured out within our hearts through the Holy Spirit who was given to us." How can this help you love your wife the way she needs to be loved?

3. Read Romans 8:5. What role does your mind play in walking by the Spirit?

4. Talk with your wife about the five love languages. What is the primary love language for each of you?

5. Talk to God about balance in your life. Do you need to make any adjustments?

6. Does your wife know she's your top priority? How do you show

her she's a top priority? Ask her how often she feels like your top priority (if you're ready for an honest answer).

7. Can you identify any flesh patterns in your life? One easy way to identify them is to consider how you react when you are hurt, angry, stressed, or tired.

8. Ask your wife how you can help her. Invite her to make a "Things You Can Do for Me Anytime" list. This week, be sure to do one thing on her list.

9. What can you do in the next week to love your wife in a romantic way?

10. What are some of the dangers of your wife not feeling loved by you?

11. Read John 8:44 and 1 Peter 5:8. What can you do to guard and protect your marriage from Satan's attacks?

12. Review the commitments you made at the beginning of this study guide. How are you doing?

Chapter 4—He Said, She Said

1. I began this chapter by saying that many wives say their greatest

need is for their husbands to listen to them. Is this one of your wife's top needs? Have you asked her?

2. In what ways do your communication patterns with your wife encourage closeness in your marriage? In what ways do they hinder it?

3. Do you have any face-to-face communication rituals? Can you develop one or become more consistent in this ritual?

4. What's the difference between listening and hearing? What can you do to practice hearing your wife's emotions as well as her words? Does your wife feel as if you really hear her?

5. In what ways does your body language encourage closeness? In what ways does it hinder closeness? Women repeatedly told me that they felt ignored when their husbands continued watching TV or looking at the computer during conversations. Do you step away from distractions when talking to your wife?

6. Proverbs provides numerous guidelines for how we should speak in a godly manner. Look up each of these verses and write down what you learn about talking:

   Proverbs 16:24

   Proverbs 17:27-28

   Proverbs 18:1-2

   Proverbs 18:21

7. Ephesians 4:26 tells us to "be angry, and yet do not sin; do not let the sun go down on your anger." How can you put this into practice?

8. Read Ephesians 4:29-32. List at least six helpful things to say. List six things that would not be helpful to say.

9. How have you offered your wife the gift of encouragement and praise?

10. Read James 5:16. According to this verse, how can we bring healing to our marriage?

11. Read the love verses in 1 Corinthians 13:4-8. How can you apply these verses as you communicate with your wife?

12. Review the lists of words of life and words of death at the end of the chapter. Which ones can you say to your wife this week? Do you need to stop saying anything to your wife?

13. Are you having a daily quiet time with God?

Chapter 5—You *Can* Understand Your Wife

1. Read 1 Peter 3:7. What are husbands commanded to do, and what's the consequence? What insights about understanding does Proverbs 18:2 offer?

2. How is *understanding* defined in this chapter?

3. Can you think of a time when you responded to your wife with an understanding attitude? Can you think of a time when you did not?

4. Do you need to change any behavior if you are to respect your wife's femininity?

5. Read the following three Scriptures. Write down what God says about our thoughts.

   Proverbs 23:7

   Romans 12:2

   2 Corinthians 10:5

6. Use the following Scriptures as prayers for your wife to be rooted and established in God's Word. Find other Scriptures and personalize them as prayers for your wife.

   _____ *is His workmanship, created in Christ Jesus for good works, which God prepared beforehand so that she would walk in them* [see Ephesians 2:10].

   I pray that from Your glorious, unlimited resources You will empower _____ with inner strength through Your Spirit. Make Your home in her heart as she trusts in You. May her roots grow down into Your love and keep her strong. And may _____ have the power to understand, as all Your people should, how wide, how long, how high, and how deep Your love is. May she experience the love of Christ, though it is too great to understand fully.

Then _____ *will be made complete with all the*
fullness of life and power that comes from You [see Ephesians 3:16-19 NLT].

_____ *can do all things through Christ who*
strengthens her [see Philippians 4:13].

7. What can you say to your wife today to assure her that she's beautiful to you?

8. How do you respond to your wife when she's emotional? What
   words or actions make her feel assured that you understand her?
   Pray about this and ask your wife about it.

9. Can you identify your personality type and your wife's? Talk to
   your wife, sharing ways you can work on accepting one another.

10. How do you respond to your wife's quirks?

11. "In the same way, the husband who wants to give up, who wants
    to say it's too hard, who wants his wife to be the one to change,
    who even thinks about walking out—that man is not the real
    you. The real you is the person God created you to be. A man
    who hungers and thirsts for God, a man who continues to seek
    God and to be transformed by the Holy Spirit from the inside
    out. I love the way The Message confirms this: 'We see the origi-
    nal and intended shape of our lives there in him' (Romans 8:29
    MSG). You discover the real you as you abide in Christ." What are
    your thoughts about this passage?

12. Are you praying for your wife daily?

Chapter 6—Attitude Adjustment

1. List the six attitudes your wife needs you to have as discussed in this chapter. Which of the attitudes is easiest for you to show your wife? Which is most difficult?

2. Have any other attitudes come to mind that your wife needs from you?

3. When was the last time you sincerely admitted to your wife you were wrong and that you were sorry? What is the commandment God gives you in James 5:16?

4. Look up the following verses about each of the attitudes discussed in this chapter. Memorize a verse that helps keep your attitude in check.

   Proverbs 17:22

   Matthew 7:1-5

   Galatians 5:22-23

   Ephesians 2:8-9

   Ephesians 4:32

   1 Thessalonians 5:16-18

   James 4:6

   1 Peter 3:7-9

5. Are your attitudes in marriage more like a stench or an aroma? Explain.

6. Read 1 Corinthians 11:11 and Galatians 6:9. How is each of these verses relevant to the attitudes you show your wife?

7. In what ways is God using your marriage to refine your character? What impurities is God sifting from your life?

8. What is your response to the question I asked in this chapter: "What if a stranger observed you only in your marriage relationship? What would this stranger discover about you?"

9. I mentioned Proverbs 21:1 in an earlier chapter: "The king's heart is like channels of water in the hand of the LORD; He turns it wherever He wishes." Are you keeping your heart and marriage surrendered to the Lord?

10. Are you involved in a church or a men's group? Do you have a good male friend who holds you accountable in your walk with the Lord?

11. Have you prayed for your wife and your marriage today?

Chapter 7—Share the Journey

1. What does sharing the journey of life with your wife mean to you? What does it mean to your wife?

2. What does being a provider mean to you to? How have you lived out this definition?

3. Read the following verses: What do you learn about money?

   Proverbs 3:9-10

   Proverbs 10:16

   Proverbs 11:4

   Ecclesiastes 5:8-15

   1 Timothy 6:6-12

4. Read Proverbs 6:6-11 and 12:11. What do you learn about work?

5. Do you have a balanced work and family life? What does your wife say? How can the following Scriptures guide you in balancing your priorities?

   Proverbs 3:5-6

   Proverbs 11:1

   Ecclesiastes 3:1

6. Talk to your wife about the household chores. Does she feel as if you are partners in this area? Here's a big challenge: Ask your wife what her least favorite chore is. Can that become your chore for a day, a week, or forever?

7. What is your family's personality? Does it reflect your wife's priorities and values as well as your own?

8. Name two of your strengths as a father. Name two of your weaknesses. Ask your wife and your children to identify two of your strengths and two of your weaknesses as a father.

9. What legacy are you leaving your children?

10. How do you support your wife's interests or dreams?

11. What can you do today to make your wife feel as if you're on her team?

12. Have you prayed for your wife and children today?

Chapter 8—Kids, Kitchen, and Kissing

1. This would be a great chapter to discuss with your wife. You might even ask her to read the chapter. Use this study guide to generate conversations with your wife.

2. What are some positives aspects of your sex life? What are some challenges? Ask your wife the same questions.

3. Ask your wife to name three ways you make her feel loved.

4. Read Ephesians 5:25-33. In what ways do you love your wife the way Christ loves the church? Have you made improvements as you've read this book?

5. When's the last time you were affectionate with your wife without expecting sex? Is nonsexual touching important to your wife?

6. How do you help your wife to make a mental adjustment so she's more ready to be sexually intimate?

7. Do you know what arouses your wife sexually? Can you and your wife have an honest conversation about this?

8. Have you ever been stuck in the "what comes first" rut? Can you take the high road and be the one to get out of this rut? What does that mean you need to do?

9. Have you violated the commitment you have to your wife with your thoughts, eyes, or actions?

10. Do you need to confess (to God and to your wife) any sexual impurity?

11. What boundaries do you have to guard and protect your marriage? Have you and your wife had a conversation specifically about this?

12. Read the following Scriptures and make a note of how they can help with your sex life.

    Matthew 5:27-30

    1 Corinthians 7:4

    1 Corinthians 13:5

    Galatians 5:17-25

    Ephesians 5:3

    James 5:16

13. How are you doing at seeking the Lord first in your life?

Chapter 9—For Better or for Worse

1. Have you weathered a storm in your marriage? How did it affect your marriage?

2. What does a heavenly perspective entail? How can this help you during a storm?

3. Read each of the following verses. Write down the promises God gives you for going through hard times.

    Exodus 14:13-14

    Psalm 37:3-6

    Psalm 40:1-3

    Isaiah 43:1-2

    1 Corinthians 13:4-7

    Colossians 1:17

    Hebrews 5:8

4. During stressful times, do you and your wife turn toward one another, away from one another, or against one another?

5. What's the difference between being thankful *for* a situation and being thankful *in* a situation?

6. What is your reaction to Brooke and Russ's story and to Erica and Pete's? What do you learn from their stories?

7. Read Romans 5:3-5. What are some of the results of tribulations?

8. How do you guard your heart against unfaithfulness?

9. Do you have boundaries in place to protect your marriage from sexual temptations?

10. Read Psalm 66:10-12. Meditate on the beauty of this affirmation.

11. Have you had a quiet time lately?

Chapter 10—The Treasure of a Wife

1. Read Philippians 1:6. What promise do you find in this verse, and how can you apply it to your marriage?

2. Read Philippians 3:12-14 (msg): "I'm not saying that I have this all together, that I have it made. But I am well on my way, reaching out for Christ, who has so wondrously reached out for me. Friends, don't get me wrong: By no means do I count myself an

expert in all of this, but I've got my eye on the goal, where God is beckoning us onward—to Jesus. I'm off and running, and I'm not turning back." What can you relate to in these verses? What do they make you think of concerning your marriage?

3. Read James 1:17. List some of the reasons your marriage is one of the good things given to you from God.

4. Has your marriage changed as you've read and applied the principles in this book? In what ways?

5. Consider asking your wife what changes she's seen in you. Ask her if there's a change she'd still like to see in your marriage.

6. In an earlier chapter I wrote, "As you become the man God wants you to be, you'll also become the husband your wife needs." Have you found this statement to be true? Explain.

7. List two or three things you want to take away from reading this book.

Notes

~~~

Chapter 1: The Starting Point

1. Gary Smalley, *Hidden Keys of a Loving, Lasting Marriage* (Grand Rapids: Zondervan, 1984), 40-41.

Chapter 2: Be the Man

1. Gary Chapman, in *The Transformation of a Man's Heart,* ed. by Stephen W. Smith (Downers Grove, IL: InterVarsity Press, 2006), 142-43.

2. Steve and Annie Chapman, *What Husbands and Wives Aren't Telling Each Other* (Eugene, OR: Harvest House, 2003), 134.

3. Stormie Omartian, *The Power of a Praying Husband* (Eugene, OR: Harvest House, 2001), 25.

Chapter 3: Love Her No Matter What

1. Gary Chapman, *The Five Love Languages* (Chicago: Northfield, 1992), 135.

Chapter 4: He Said, She Said

1. Bill and Pam Farrell, *Men Are Like Waffles—Women Are Like Spaghetti* (Eugene, OR: Harvest House, 2001), 11, 13.

2. Gary Thomas, *Sacred Marriage* (Grand Rapids: Zondervan, 2006), 10.

Chapter 5: You *Can* Understand Your Wife

1. Florence Littauer, *Personality Plus for Couples* (Grand Rapids: Revell, 2001), 19.
2. Littauer, *Personality Plus for Couples,* 20.
3. Littauer, *Personality Plus for Couples,* 21.

Chapter 8: Kids, Kitchen, and Kissing

1. Kevin Lehman, *Sheet Music* (Carol Stream, IL: Tyndale House, 2003), 273-74.
2. Gary Thomas, *Sacred Marriage* (Grand Rapids: Zondervan, 2000), 216.
3. Lysa TerKeurst, *Capture Her Heart* (Chicago: Moody Press, 2002), 119-20.
4. Tim and Beverly LaHaye, *The Act of Marriage* (Grand Rapids: Zondervan, 1976), 141.
5. Lehman, *Sheet Music,* 59.

Chapter 9: For Better or for Worse

1. Adapted from Curt and Marybeth Whalen, *Learning to Live Financially Free* (Grand Rapids: Kregel, 2009).

Melanie Chitwood is a writer, teacher, and speaker living in Charlotte, North Carolina. To contact her for speaking engagements, visit her website and blog at www.melaniechitwood.com or contact Proverbs 31 Ministries at www.proverbs31.org. You can also e-mail Melanie at melandtheboys@gmail.com.

From Melanie Chitwood to Your Wife...

WHAT A HUSBAND NEEDS FROM HIS WIFE

What does your husband *really* need from you? And what is the best way for you to meet those needs? This engaging and thoroughly biblical guide demonstrates that you meet your husband's needs most effectively by maintaining your own vibrant personal relationship with Christ. Filled with useful tools that will help you understand your husband better, this enlightening resource includes...

- ideas for dealing with addictions, infidelity, and financial challenges

- explanations of personality types and love languages

- resources that offer help for the helper

A study guide at the end of the book makes this a perfect tool for individual or small group use.